COVER OF DARKNESS

Cover of Darkness

———— ✴ ————

RODERICK CHISHOLM
C.B.E., D.S.O., D.F.C.

With a Foreword by
Air Chief Marshal
SIR WILLIAM ELLIOT
K.C.B., K.B.E., D.F.C.

1953
CHATTO & WINDUS
LONDON

PUBLISHED BY
Chatto & Windus
LONDON

★

Clarke, Irwin & Co. Ltd.
TORONTO

To the memory of
FLYING OFFICER W. G. RIPLEY, D.F.M.
FLYING OFFICER N. L. BAMFORD, D.F.C.
FLIGHT LIEUTENANT F. C. CLARKE
who flew with me and brought about
the successes I describe—and to the
crews of Bomber Command

FOREWORD

by Air Chief Marshal Sir William Elliot

K.C.B., K.B.E., D.F.C.

Cover of Darkness is essentially a book about the air
by an airman. It has nothing to do with the land or
the sea.

It is a chapter in the history of the war, threading
its way through the battle in the air at night, which
began over Great Britain and ended over Germany.
It is also a chapter in the history of our country. We
know, though we are reluctant to admit it, that
we have lost our integral insular security. That insular security, in which we were so long enfolded by
the seas around us, has now been dispersed into the
air, not only above, but far beyond those seas. To
defend ourselves we must fly. If these changed circumstances give us cause for anxiety, they equally present
us with a challenge such as any great people is proud
to accept. They have already given us the opportunity
of adding a prowess in airfaring to our heritage of
seafaring.

The achievements which this book describes were
founded in the art of flying. This is an art which is as
fine as it is exacting; and one which demands of those
who practise it high qualities of mind and body and
character—in particular those which Mr. Winston
Churchill has described as "the canine virtues; vigil-
ance, fidelity, courage and love of the chase."

The author, and many of those whom he mentions,

were known to me. I know that both he and they would wish me to say that they were typical, and not exceptional, of all those young Englishmen who did what they did bravely and competently in the daily round of defending their country. "We, the aircrew," he says, "were happily unconscious of the bigger issues, and our only anxieties outside our own flying tasks were such seemingly vital domesticities as the establishing of the right to late breakfast, the night flyer's extra egg or petrol for leave." Yes, in part; but beyond this they were assuredly not among those who were "untroubled by a spark". They knew and "prized the doubt". They understood what was at stake, and they played the game with the skill and care, the patience and the endurance, which alone brings to great adventurers great rewards.

CONTENTS

Foreword by Air Chief Marshal Sir William Elliot
K.C.B., K.B.E., D.F.C.

PART ONE: DEFENCE

PART TWO: ATTACK

CONTENTS

ILLUSTRATIONS

Part One

DEFENCE

Chapter 4

THE WAY HOME

WHEN the war began I was in Persia. Oil was my business and Tehran was my headquarters. On the day we declared war I was in Mazanderan, the Caspian province, in a small, strange seaside town called Babolsar. There was a radio in a Russo-Armenian pension, and as one of a solemn and polyglot group I heard the news and then the King. I felt, feeling relieved, my morale restored. At last it was certain what we were in for.

I hurried back to Tehran, and as I motored I made and discarded plans. Decisions had to be made, and there was no help to be got in the making of them. Hints had been dropped that I would be valuable in Persia and should remain, but I had Auxiliary Air Force affiliations and this made inevitable the easier course—to go home rather than to wait in Persia for the showdown that was bound to come there.

In Tehran I found a letter for me On His Majesty's Service, but instead of orders it conveyed only my relegation to a nondescript category of the A.A.F. Reserve. After this I took things more leisurely and made plans with some deliberation. I learnt that the decision had to be mine and that I could return to my Squadron if I applied. This I did and, having been passed fit for flying by the R.A.F. doctors at headquarters Iraq, I had not long to wait for a cable instructing me to

Chapter 1

THE WAY HOME

WHEN the war began I was in Persia. Oil was my business and Teheran was my headquarters. On the day we declared war I was in Mazanderan, the Caspian province, in a small, strange seaside town called Babolsar. There was a radio in a Russo-Armenian *pension*, and as one of a solemn and polyglot group I heard the news and then the King. I left, feeling relieved, my morale restored. At last it was certain what we were in for.

I hurried back to Teheran, and as I motored I made and discarded plans. Decisions had to be made, and there was no help to be got in the making of them. Hints had been dropped that I would be valuable in Persia and should remain, but I had Auxiliary Air Force affiliations and this made inevitable the easier course—to go home rather than to wait in Persia for the showdown that was bound to come there.

In Teheran I found a letter for me On His Majesty's Service, but instead of orders it conveyed only my relegation to a non-flying category of the A.A.F. Reserve. After this I took things more leisurely and made plans with some deliberation. I learnt that the decision had to be mine and that I could return to my Squadron if I applied. This I did and, having been passed fit for flying by the R.A.F. doctors at headquarters Iraq, I had not long to wait for a cable instructing me to return home and report to the Air Ministry.

I left Teheran in January in a snow-storm. By then all had been completed. My worldly goods, the accumulation of five years' independent self-indulgence, had been sold or stored and I had handed over my work to a successor. It all sounded trivial as I explained it to him item by item; and yet, when it was my work and when there was no war to be thought of, it had often seemed of the utmost importance. It was sad to say good-bye to my friends and to be leaving a country which I had grown to like and where, on the whole, I had been happy.

I had been fortunate to have worked for the three past years in Teheran. There the life had been interesting, gay and, on looking back, a little exotic; and the work had been satisfying, absorbing and carefree. In our office a wise and considerate management had fostered a congenial atmosphere, and the happy relationship between the Persians and British seemed to bring out the best in both.

I made my way to London by Abadan, Baghdad, Damascus, Beirut, Venice, Paris, Calais and Dover. As I went west, the weather became worse and the gloom deeper. I stayed a few days at Beirut, where the sun was still shining, and a day in Paris, where it was wet and cold; many restaurants there were closed because the waiters had been called up, and there was only a feeble attempt at blackout. London, it was explained, would surely be bombed first.

There was a crescendo in formalities and precautions and waiting. Fog in the Channel kept me for two impatient days and nights on an overcrowded steamer in Calais harbour, and even after an uneventful dash across the Channel there was for me and other civilians a three-hour wait before disembarking.

Apart from uniforms and the blackout, there seemed to be few changes in London, and I began to doubt the wisdom of coming home for what then seemed a 'phoney' war. I acquired a civilian identity-card and ration-book, and I went to the Air Ministry, where I eventually found my goal at the end of a dusty passage. I went in and unburdened myself to a sympathetic squadron leader. I learnt that I was still acceptable for operations (in those days there were rumours that pilots in the late twenties were too old) and that I could go back to my Squadron, but that I would have to have a refresher course. When would I be ready to go on it? I said I was ready at once. No, I wanted no leave. I would be told when and where to report.

It was not until February 23rd that I reported at a place called South Cerney.

Chapter 2

LEARNING TO FLY AGAIN

WEARING my only uniform and with the barest essentials in my suitcase, I arrived eventually at the sleepy market-town terminus of a single line. A smart van took me the few miles to the camp.

At once I seemed nearer the war. My imagination ran away. I saw myself now nearly combatant. Life had become suddenly very exciting and every item of it was interesting. I would soon begin to understand how my war would start. I did not take much interest in what happened thereafter, for at least there were no anxieties about a future and no need for foresight.

This was a new peace of mind, and I was content and resigned. The cause was worthwhile, and life, while it continued, would be as exciting as its end, when it came, would be sudden. It was comforting, too, that there would be no soldiering, for which I had maintained a revulsion since my time in a school O.T.C. War as a soldier I saw as a continuation in grim earnest of the series of field days that I had detested so cordially at O.T.C. camps. And to the squalor and discomfort of those make-believe battles there would be added fright, as before a football match, but magnified a thousandfold and perpetual; there would also be the gore, gas and inescapable dirt.

War as an airman was a different proposition. I pictured to myself a prolonged Auxiliary Air Force camp such as I had enjoyed at Tangmere in the early 'thirties. Well away from the trenches, we would live gaily under canvas or in comfortable billets. We would mess well and, not being cannon-fodder, we would be conscious all the time of our part in the plan of battle. There would be the grimness of war, but it would be tempered by the beauty of the setting of the air war. We would fly all day, from first to last light. We would take part in those dawn and dusk patrols that were so glamourised after the first war, and we would be the privileged spectators of scenes defying description in their beauty and impossible for the earthbound to picture and understand.

In 1930, when I joined the Auxiliary Air Force, I had been influenced by this idea of war. I had reckoned then that it would be infinitely preferable to go to war in the air than on the ground, and in February 1940 I was certain that the choice, for me, had been right.

To school I went, prepared for hard living and reconciled to the prospect of an austere life; but instead of a tent or a place in a hut dormitory, I was given a room to myself in a comfortable mess, for South Cerney was a large, recently built, permanent station.

When someone broke into the isolation which is the newcomer's lot in most R.A.F. messes and asked me what I was doing there, I replied that I had come to join Course 31 to have refresher training, and in particular to learn to fly twins. I was told that pilots of Course 31 had just left I.T.S. and were going to A.T.S. I knew nothing then about the training organisation, and I asked what were the E.F.T.S., S.F.T.S., I.T.S., A.T.S. and O.T.U., of which I had heard but whose significance was as yet unknown to me.

I learnt that embryo pilots went first to an elementary flying training school (E.F.T.S.) for basic instruction on a simple type such as the Tiger Moth, and thence to the Service F.T.S. to fly a more advanced type such as the Oxford, to study the ancillary subjects and then to apply them in practice. The first part was in the Intermediate Training Squadron (I.T.S.), where they learnt to fly the advanced trainer and followed simultaneously an intensive course of lectures on engines, airframes, bombing, gunnery, armament, signals, navigation, airmanship and all the rest of it. After passing out of I.T.S. by reaching the necessary standard in flying and in the lecture subjects, they were awarded their wings and graduated to the Advanced Training Squadron (A.T.S.). There they would endeavour to put theory into practice under the general headings of fighting, bombing and reconnoitring.

The course at the S.F.T.S. lasted four months, and at the end of it pilots were posted direct to squadrons or to Operational Training Units (O.T.U.) for further training. In the latter units, then in their infancy, they flew aircraft of operational type and, where appropriate to their rôle, were joined by others to make a crew. On leaving for their squadrons, pilots and crews were assumed to be up to operational standard, thus —in theory at least—relieving the squadron of all further training but the final polish.

Mid-course examinations had begun for Course 31,

and the literal official interpretation of my situation was that I must sit for them with the course I was joining. I attended the first, but finding morse at eleven words a minute beyond me—I knew no morse whatever—I left and sought out the chief flying instructor. He soon discovered the shortcomings of my flying experience—that I had never flown a twin, never flown at night, and that in the last five years I had only done a very few hours. When I left him I had been put into Course 32 to start from the beginning; I would be there for four months. The war seemed to be receding.

I had to start right from the beginning, and it was explained to me by a stern flight-commander instructor that I was not to forget that I was a pupil and that I must 'toe the line', as he put it. Thus I was put in my place with the pupils, a great way off from the instructors who, though mostly of like or lower rank and (it seemed from their baby faces) junior in years to me, had to be saluted punctiliously and invariably addressed as 'Sir'. As an auxiliary I doubted whether flying instruction was best given in an atmosphere suggesting the parade ground, and I wondered whether all this was really necessary.

Otherwise I had little to complain of. I was spared having to march from the mess to the hangars every morning, and in the mess I was accorded the somewhat dubious privilege of using the staff anteroom: a privilege whose use often persuaded me to retire to my room to study the mysteries of bomb-aiming, navigation, pyrotechnics and kindred subjects.

With trepidation I went solo in an Oxford. I did

not expect to enjoy the flying at first, not until I had some confidence, and I found that this confidence came slowly. Being frightened I was cautious, but in the hands of a mature and even-tempered instructor, a real master of a rare art, I made slow but sure progress. He concentrated on the fundamentals, believing that first I must learn to fly safely and that the polish would come later—a view with which I wholeheartedly agreed. He was typical of many of the pre-war non-commissioned officers of the R.A.F., permanent and essential struts in the Service's slender peace-time structure.

It was particularly cheering in May 1940, when the mythically invulnerable French army was retreating in disorder, to hear the N.C.O. instructor's views on the war, our allies and their probable value, our opponents actual and prospective, and the certainty of our victory, a quick victory at that.

On the day when the newspapers reported the breakthrough at Sedan, described as 'the bulge' and illustrated by maps showing an imaginary line where, one guessed, no line of any sort existed, a typical comment was "Wait and see. We'll wait till that gets a bit bigger and then we'll nip it off." And the next day when the bulge was ominously larger the comment was: "We're luring them on, and when they're all in the bulge we'll have 'em all in the bag. That's tactics."

And the reaction, crude, cockney and prophetic, to the news that Mussolini, still officially a neutral, had made a threatening speech about Mare Nostrum was: "Musso! No'ing but piss and wind! Tyke awiy 'is spaghetti an' 'e'd croy loike a baiby." Such morale is unbreakable, and luckily it is infectious.

There was, I soon found, a great and profound peace of mind in a regular and disciplined existence. My days were full; I knew where I had to be, what I had to do and when I had to do it. The work was interesting, and since I was an officer alone in a course of sergeants, all of them younger than me and in intense competition for commissions, I had to work hard to avoid disgracing myself. I took the lectures and other ground instruction very seriously, for I was keen to be assessed as at least 'average'. I discovered that my mind was rusty, and that my ability to concentrate, which had never been great, had dwindled depressingly.

In the flying I had gone solo and I was making progress; but I had an inferiority complex and it took time to get over it. The first, hard-won self-confidence required careful nursing, and my progress was not without setbacks; for although my own instructor was in every way the ideal instructor for me, there were others who, unknowingly, nearly undid all the good he did.

Like the incivilities of the hunting field or the abuse exchanged by motorists, the petulance of pilots when airborne is a not abnormal reaction to the stresses of a potentially dangerous pursuit. Most of us will probably react that way, and systems and people should respect our failings. Pilots when flying should be treated as children; many of them want soothing, inspiring and sometimes gentle coaxing; all of them will respond to considerate treatment. I have the conviction that several of those I knew who failed and never became pilots might have succeeded had they been, as I was, in the right hands. That need for sympathetic understanding went much further than flying instruction; it was as great between controller and pilot in operations as between pupil and instructor in training.

In a situation I remember, it was probably the timely arrival on duty of a particular controller which saved lives: the weather had turned bad when, after a patrol of some hours, a Beaufighter came back to land. It had not much petrol left, and the visibility near the ground was bad and deteriorating rapidly. The pilot made two attempts to land, but both had been frustrated by the mist which was thickening and which, when seen obliquely, obliterated the flare-path lights. He was flustered and probably he was becoming panicky; he might have attempted a crash landing —there is an urge, which can become overwhelming when panic takes hold, to get down quickly and anyhow on to terra firma—but Peter [1] came on duty and took over. We all knew and had a great regard for Peter. He dealt calmly with the situation and, speaking quietly, he told the pilot simply to climb up to a good height and bale out, and he added in his own way and with his own idiom, which we all knew and could instantly recognise, "See that you do it prettily because there is a large audience", or some such phrase, flippant but wholly appropriate to the situation. The pilot regained confidence; he knew that voice and he understood the message. He climbed to ten thousand and he and his observer 'stepped out', as we used to say.

[1] Wing Commander P. B. Robinson.

Contrast Peter's way with that of another with whom, one night, I had the following exchange:

I. "What is my position?"

He. "You are over point four." (Point four on the line I was patrolling.)

I. "What is my distance and bearing from base?"

He. "You should know."

He was quite right. I should have known and doubtless my ignorance merited comment and reproof; but at the right time, and this was certainly not it. I had been flying in a Blenheim for more than two hours on an uneventful patrol. It was pitch dark and bitterly cold at 20,000 feet—the heating seldom worked in Blenheims—and the boredom and cold had reduced my morale to a low ebb. The ground was obscured by cloud, and the chance of radio failure, in those days, was appreciable. It was therefore a comforting and wise precaution often to check distances and bearings back to base so that in case of some breakdown there would be a reasonable chance of getting back. That his reply had nettled me was a minor matter. I should have laughed it off, though that was hard to do in the circumstances, nervous as I was, icy cold and in the dark three to four miles high (and I could not forget that he was in a warm, light and supposedly bombproof operations-room). A major and far more serious result was that my nervous stability was unsettled and my efficiency impaired. Petulance must be the prerogative of the pilot. It takes very little to ruin a controller's reputation.

I was sharply (and painfully) reminded of the ill

effects that rough treatment by instructors can have even during a period of retraining (I was, after all, not a beginner). I had attained that stage in my flying when I had to pass a test; I had to show my flight-commander how I flew and to be assessed by him. It was he who had told me on my arrival that I had to 'toe the line'. He was accepted as an expert and very polished pilot, and he was sick to death of instructing.

I was apprehensive about my prospects, nervous and anxious to do well, and early on I made a small but not dangerous mistake. I was questioned testily about what I had been taught, and I replied briefly and with some confusion. Here, it seemed, I made a worse mistake and I was soundly dressed down. I might well be a Flying Officer (and he was a Flight Lieutenant), but I had, at all times, to address him as 'Sir'. I should have laughed at him (afterwards this exchange seemed only laughable, for we were sitting side by side and this lecture on deportment was delivered through a microphone), but I could not; I was too rattled. My flying went from bad to worse; I had lost all self-confidence. I was humiliated and furious.

After landing, I asked him not to worry about my feelings. He had found me out; he had succeeded in rattling me. What could I be expected to do in the face of the enemy if I had done this under the influence of a personality? I would be disappointed at being failed, but his duty was to fail me; I would be able to find myself other employment without any difficulty. He tried to reassure me; he was apologetic about being bad tempered; he said he was tired. He would give me another test in a few days.

Later we flew together again, and this time he hardly spoke. I performed all right, but I felt all the time as if I was walking a tight-rope. I had precious little self-confidence then, even though some days had elapsed since that first test.

This was a real crisis in my flying and it was narrowly survived. In the recounting it sounds petty but at the time its importance was very great. It made me wonder how many new pupil pilots are made into failures by incorrect psychological handling during their training. I had four hundred hours' flying to my credit already and yet I was reduced to the hopeless and dangerous state of no confidence. Perhaps I was over-sensitive, but good flying instruction must cater for all types. It is a great and rare art.

After this incident I did not look back. I progressed from the Intermediate to the Advanced Squadron, and in the examinations I did not disgrace myself.

*

The first night solo was the greatest event in my training. To be launched into the dark by oneself for the first time is a greater adventure than the first daylight solo. Most of us have an instinctive dislike of the dark and one knows before trying that flying in the dark will be more exacting than flying in daylight.

Night-flying training took a heavy toll and the obvious causes were few; one could usually only guess why this or that disaster had come about. Some small routine matter might have gone wrong, causing a momentary loss of equilibrium; control might have been regained or panic might have taken charge. Or too much dependence might have been placed on sensations of movement which, divorced from visual aid, were only misleading. There were plenty of pit-falls.

I had done the normal amount of instrument flying and I had learnt how sensations can deceive. The pressure on a seat can suggest a turn, a climb or a dive, and all the time the instruments may show that something quite different is happening. To learn that these sensations had, to a large extent, to be ignored was one thing; to succeed in ignoring them was going to be much harder.

When I first flew at night it was moonless and very dark. The take-off and landing run (there were no runways then) were marked by paraffin-flares laid out to form a very elongated tee. There was no floodlight and one had to touch down by the light of the aircraft's landing-lamp. I flew with my instructor for about an hour, practising circuits, take-offs and landings. Under his competent supervision I went through all the motions of night flying. I took off, climbed to about a thousand feet with my eyes glued to the instruments, turned left through ninety degrees, flew on for about a minute, turned left again through another ninety degrees and, when straightened out, glanced out hoping to see the flare-path over the left side. I saw it, signalled for permission to land and, getting a 'green', turned in to approach to land. Given a 'red' I had to go round again, doing gentle turns at the corners, concentrating on the instruments as much as

I was able, and glancing out now and again to regain visual touch with the ground and the aerodrome circuit. Approaching to land, I did my last turn so as to face along the flare-path at about five hundred feet. I had put the wheels down before this turn, and I waited until I had straightened out to put the flaps down. I throttled back and tried to keep my eyes on two things at once, the air-speed indicator and the flare-path. At about a hundred feet I put on the landing-light. The ground came into focus and then came up as if to hit me. A nervous motion closed the throttles and pulled back the stick—too suddenly—and the flattening out was overdone. I eased the stick forward and the machine sailed on and on, getting lower and slower. Then there was a sickening bump and a series of decreasing bumps. Stick back and brakes on and it was all over. That was the procedure; there were sufficient rules for a safe night circuit and landing. All I had to do was to repeat the performance without the steadying influence of my instructor's presence.

When he said: "Well, that seemed to go all right. What do you think about it? Do you feel like going solo?" I nearly said I would prefer to have a little more practice because I was not very confident. Yet I reckoned that I would never become more confident until I had been solo. There were certain steps in flying which have to be jumped, and this was one. Then I heard that another member of the Course had just gone solo, and so there was no question; I had to try.

All went as it should, and I had hardly an anxious moment, though when I had taxied in and tried to get out I found that my knees were weak. But I was relieved and supremely happy.

The first cross-country at night is the most hazardous step in flying experience. Risks which were measurable in daylight and soon forgotten become immeasurably greater in the dark and harder to forget. The dark is exacting; a radio failure, an engine failure or an error in navigation can precipitate a crisis from which the only sure way out is by parachute. And with this knowledge a pilot is, at first, an easy prey to panic. Panic is always there, ready to take charge, to prevent him from thinking clearly, to urge him soon to set aside one plan of action and try another, and although it can be suppressed by constant practice, it is, I think, never finally overcome.

My first night cross-country came some time after leaving the F.T.S. It was very short, unpremeditated and, although a good enough story afterwards, very frightening. I was to do 'circuits and bumps', and because there were several of us doing the same thing I was kept waiting, signalling for permission to land but ignored, for about half an hour. I was anything but composed, and when a turn proved too much for the directional gyro, which spun, I also lost my sense of direction.

At last I was given a 'green', but the dim pattern of aerodrome lights made little sense by this time, and my approach to land was not aligned with the flare-path, whose direction I understood too late. I had to go round again. The wheels and flaps on a Blenheim came up rather slowly, and by the time I was ready to start a circuit I knew that I was several miles from the aerodrome; but I could not picture my position, and the lights which I could see did nothing but confuse me. I was flustered, and the situation suddenly got out of hand. I did not know where I was; therefore I was lost. A feeling of panic came over me, and I could not think of anything except getting down somehow on to terra firma. It must be this paralysis that causes the inexplicable night-flying accidents. It took a great effort for common sense to overcome this one instinct, which seemed still to work, to return to earth as soon as possible; but slowly this happened and item by item things were checked. What height? What speed? Climbing or diving? Where was I likely to be? Each of these checks, usually done instinctively and instantaneously, now needed a special effort.

I was too low; I must climb so that I could see the beacons. I climbed unsteadily to two thousand feet. Bit by bit the crisis passed and confidence returned. The night was clear and I knew I could not be far from base. It was only necessary to keep my head.

This is what was then going through my mind; this is the shameful performance of the uninitiated: "There's a beacon—what's it flashing?—dot something, missed it—climbing too steeply—must level out —now where's that beacon again?—get the beacon paper—(it's too flimsy)—where's the torch?—mustn't get flustered again—there's plenty of time—climbing again—must level out—Andover VL, Wallop DA— now where's the beacon?—there it is—think clearly, read it slowly—looks like a V then L, that's certain— read it again—there it goes again: it's Andover— about 240 degrees for Wallop—settle down, align the gyro—steady—lights ahead—a beacon—flashing DA —that's Wallop—this is simple—I could go on, I'd like to go on now—this will be a joke to-morrow."

I believe that experiences like these were common enough; I suspect that most pilots have, at one time, felt what I felt.

Chapter 3

BACK IN THE FOLD

ON June 15th, 1940, my Course was posted away. The last few days at F.T.S. were as vivid and significant as the last few days at school or any other milestone in my life. I believed then, as other members of the Course believed, that we were going straight to war. I had been informed politely by the C.O. of my Squadron that he hoped I would not come back without adequate training, and he suggested that I should go to an Operational Training Unit to learn to fly a Blenheim before rejoining. But another view prevailed and I got instructions to report at Manston after a week's leave.

Conscious of being free from worries and anxieties, I went to London, soon sickened of it, and with relief went north to Ampleforth to meet my mother. Ampleforth then seemed more beautiful than it had ever been before. The repose and unworldliness of a monastery distracted my thoughts for a short while from a world which seemed mad, and surroundings which I had met first when I was seven and which I had unwittingly learnt to love, proved generous compensation for the barrenness of the foreign scene of the past five years. A Yorkshire valley which had meant little to me as a schoolboy seemed, in June 1940, the most beautiful place I had ever seen. The evenings—they reminded me of ratting at the farm instead of cricket practice—were still and clear, and the colours were strangely vivid and changed, as if seen through tinted glasses. I was happy and contented. Being in the grip of the machine, I felt I could do no more and was at peace with myself.

604 Squadron had moved to Northolt, and there I joined it. I found some faces I knew vaguely but very few that I knew well, for it was five years since I had left and most of my contemporaries had been dispersed to other squadrons and jobs. The complement was, however, still largely auxiliary, and as an old member of the Squadron returned from exile, I was at once made to feel at home.

I learnt that the Squadron's operations were now restricted to night-fighter patrols, the Blenheim bomber —turned fighter by adding four machine-guns beneath the fuselage—having proved itself by costly experience totally inadequate as a day-fighter over western Europe. Mike Anderson,[1] the C.O. (he and I had joined the Squadron on the same day ten years before) explained that the dual Blenheim was away, being equipped with what he described as 'magic mirrors', and so I would not be able to have any instruction for a week or two. In the meantime I would be sent on a course to learn something about fighter-control methods and tactics.

I went on the course, and found it ingenious, instructive and highly diverting. The pupil pilots themselves took the parts of fighter and bomber pilot and fighter controller in a simplified, slow and practical

[1] Wing Commander M. F. Anderson, D.F.C.

34

demonstration of principle and practice. The stage had one dimension less than in real life, and instead of the limitless vault of the heavens it was the grass centre of a sports stadium. Aircraft became tricycles equipped with metronomes (to control pedalling speed), radios, compasses and screens, behind which the pupil pilots pedalled blindly and obediently on compass bearings and at speeds ordained by the controller and passed to them by radio. The controller was out of view, in an operations room which had once been a changing room at the back of the stadium, and the positions of the bomber and fighter tricycles were reported by spotters high up in the stands. The conditions were partly realistic and learning was easy; on a balmy summer's day it was also great fun.

Blenheim fighters were being used on night operations for another reason besides their inadequacy as fighters in daylight. Some far-sighted people, realising the need for specialisation in night defence, had prevailed in the planning councils, and in June 1940 we found our Blenheims being fitted with Mike's 'magic mirrors'.

This equipment consisted of a radio transmitter and receiver and the necessary aerials. From a harpoon-shaped aerial on the fighter's nose pulses were propagated in all directions (but predominantly ahead). On meeting another aircraft they were reflected, in part, back to the fighter, to be received through four directional aerials (arranged to 'look out' predominantly up, down, left and right). The echo pulses as received through each of these aerials were displayed on cathode-ray tubes, and the observer was able to judge the bearings of the echo given from the fighter by comparing their sizes. On the cathode-ray tubes the interval between emission of a pulse and its reception as an echo was also shown, and thus the range of the echo given could be deduced, the speed of radio waves being invariable.

But to us then it was only A.I.; publicly it was announced later as Radiolocation and the Americans called it RADAR (derivation: RAdio Direction And Range). There was promise of an interesting future in night fighting, but we did not know it. In those days it was not easy to imagine how one could seek out and shoot at another aircraft in the dark, and we were sceptical about the 'magic mirrors'.

Instead of the intense activity and excitement I had expected, there was the fruitless monotony of standing patrols in the dark in aircraft which were hardly faster than the few enemy bombers which were then coming over. Many of the crews had been in good flying training when the war started, and by June 1940 they were fully proficient at night flying. During those nine months, when some Auxiliary Squadrons had been covering themselves with glory, our Squadron's tasks had been limited to convoy protection and escort

In the air the 'noise' (interference) was usually worse and often the echo was less clear. Here, the echo could be from an aircraft about 9,000 feet ahead. On the elevation (left-hand) tube there is slightly more of the echo above than below the horizontal trace, while on the azimuth (right-hand) tube there is more of it on the right than the left of the vertical trace. This would show that a target aircraft was a little above and a little to the right of the fighter's fore and aft axis. The useful range depended on height, the ground echoes blotting out any aircraft echoes at ranges greater than the fighter's height (which, in the picture, could be about 18,000 feet). Reading the faces of cathode-ray tubes was a small part of the Observer's task. By description and instruction he had to get his Pilot to visual range.

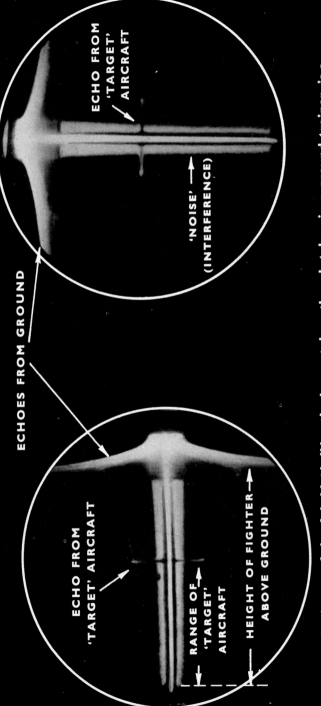

ELEVATION TUBE

AZIMUTH TUBE

ECHOES FROM GROUND

ECHO FROM 'TARGET' AIRCRAFT

'NOISE' (INTERFERENCE)

ECHO FROM 'TARGET' AIRCRAFT

RANGE OF 'TARGET' AIRCRAFT

HEIGHT OF FIGHTER ABOVE GROUND

This picture of the A.I. Mark IV cathode-ray tubes, though taken in a ground trainer, is a fair representation of what the Observer would see during an air interception in ideal conditions (See note opposite)

' Many of the crews had been in good flying
training when the war started . . .'

Reading clockwise: Philip Heal (with newspaper), John Davies,
killed on active service, Ronald Scott, John Cunningham,
Michael Anderson, Stanley Skinner, killed on active service,
Michael Doulton, killed on active service, Alastair Hunter, killed
on active service, George Budd, 'Copper' Prescott, my nephew,
killed on active service, Philip Wheeler, killed on active service.

' though it had been prepared, at one time, to go to Finland . . .'
A Squadron Blenheim in strange war paint.   In the foreground
John Selway (L), John Davies (R).

(though it had been prepared, at one time, to go to Finland), and there was an inescapable feeling of discouragement. Although I was happily absorbed in learning the job, I could not help being disappointed.

We moved to Gravesend at the beginning of July. Except for the addition of some coats of camouflage paint and the erection of a hut or two, Gravesend Airport was unchanged from peace-time, when it had a few hangars and a control-tower-cum-club-house. It was now a one-squadron station, and Mike became Station Commander. We lived in the club-house and adjoining tents. The accommodation was very crowded, but the summer was at its height and the surroundings were lovely, so no one minded. It was reminiscent of the peace-time training camps at Tangmere. My flying was restricted to daylight. I had to accustom myself to the Blenheim and to learn the thousand and one things I would have been taught at an Operational Training Unit.

A month later the Squadron was moved to a big but unfinished camp in Hampshire. It was handsome and its planning was lavish, as was the planning of all the camps which were built in those few years when the public was beginning to realise that a war was possible and the air estimates became appropriate to a first-class power; when, too, the Auxiliary Air Force was no longer debarred from flying in the vicinity of Hendon on Sunday mornings. It was a fine camp, but its concentration of buildings hardly fitted the conditions ruling in August 1940, with the enemy in France and within easy bombing range. Its name was Middle Wallop.

Chapter 4

MIDDLE WALLOP

A FEW weeks after we arrived, Middle Wallop was bombed on two consecutive afternoons with fair success. This was an experience which was depressing besides being alarming, for the short-lived and localised enemy air superiority which had permitted it suggested imminent defeat, a suggestion reassuringly dispelled by the reports of the enemy losses. This was the war, not as I had imagined it, but the war nevertheless, and although the alarm had been sounded and what followed might have been expected, I was surprised and even incredulous, momentarily, to see unidentified aircraft coming out of cloud and dropping bombs which were aimed, so it seemed, expressly at me.

On the first day that a raid came in there was cloud over the airfield, and the formations thundered awe-inspiringly overhead, hostile and unseen. I cowered obediently in a shelter that seemed to be too near the hangars, and soon made an escape to the dispersal point, where I waited, poised, ready to jump into a slit-trench. A little later the noise grew again— they were coming back—and by now the cloud had thinned and broken. I saw a machine I could not recognise, and I stood, fascinated, until out of it fell a string of harmless-looking specks which came down to burst rhythmically with resounding 'gerumphs'—by which time I was in the trench.

We climbed out of the trench to see where the damage was, and jumped back smartly as soon as another enemy was spotted. Little damage was done to the camp that day.

On the next day things happened very suddenly. Eight Junkers 88 came diving out of the sun with engines racing, and dropped their bombs neatly in and around the hangars. It was beautifully done.

We with our Blenheims had little or no chance of success, for we were too slow; but on the first day, when it seemed that all was over, we were allowed to take off. One of us shot at a Messerschmitt 110 at extreme range and claimed to have hit it, but otherwise we provided distraction only to the Hurricane and Spitfire pilots who, on that afternoon, naturally enough assumed all twin-engined aircraft to be German, with the result that one Blenheim was hit and had to land with its wheels up. The next day we had to stay on the ground, feeling useless. That was all that we saw of the daylight Battle of Britain.

I was due to fly round the sector at night before becoming operational, but such was the intensity of the raiding and shortness of the nights that practice flying was continually being cancelled. In those days there was a small margin between practice and operational flying, perhaps a number only on an operations' room board, and so my name came to appear on the operational programme, but low down so that I might have an opportunity of doing a patrol when the activity had died down. For this I would fly with an air gunner in the turret and an observer who operated the radar.

Thus I and my crew found ourselves on the night of August 16th as No. 5 on the programme with, I believed, little prospect of flying. Several patrols were sent off, and then two aircraft were reported as unserviceable for the rest of the night. We were next off. It was getting late and there were only a few more hours of darkness. I thought there would probably be no more flying, and so I lay down and tried to sleep. I must have slept because the ringing of the telephone made me come to with a start. Orders were passed for a patrol on a certain line near Bristol.

This was it. I stumbled out into the darkness. I felt scared but stoical. I could not do more than this. I could but try; and if I failed I had at least tried, and I remembered, as one does most mercifully at such moments, that one is in the hands of the Almighty. I hurried as best I could towards the aircraft, towards the torches of the ground crew who were waiting. We flew for two and a half hours in beautiful weather, came back and landed successfully at the third attempt.

The patrol was a mixture of nervous tension and great exhilaration. Bristol was being blitzed 15,000 feet below me. I saw bombs explode and anti-aircraft fire and plenty of fires, but since I was never sure of myself, of the attitude of the aircraft or of my own position, this patrol was of no potential value to our night defence.

The situation, so far as I was concerned, was never entirely under control, and when I was told that a 'bandit' was reported at 'angels ten' passing point four of my patrol line and asked whether I could see anything, I had to say that I could see nothing. I was unable to take much notice of what might be going on outside, because all my attention was concentrated on trying to keep this normally stable aircraft on an even keel. My nervous grip on the controls always tended to unsteady it by making over-corrections, and when I could relax temporarily, having won the advantage over gravity for a moment, I would be looking down for the flares which marked the patrol line. Gravity would then get the upper hand, and I would again have to pore over the instruments till they danced before my eyes. And so it went on until I was told to come home.

I was homed by radio, and my joy and relief at recognising my home beacon was mingled with surprise, because I had not yet got used to the marvels of radio and had little faith in it. I believe that once I told Ripley,[1] my radar operator, to turn on the set—the 'magic mirrors' that Mike used to refer to—but he reported at once that it was unserviceable and subsided into silence.

When on the ground again a delicious lassitude came over me, and I turned over and over in my mind the satisfying thought that I had attained the goal of becoming operational. I decided then that night flying had all the dangers of day flying without any of its enjoyment and charm, but that it made up for these shortcomings by its soul-satisfying aftermath. To have taken off, to have patrolled and to have landed safely

[1] Flying Officer W. G. Ripley, D.F.M., died of injuries received on active service, November 16th, 1943.

in the dark were causes for satisfaction—thus it remained to the end.

I was operational and I could play my part in the normal activities of the Squadron; no longer was there the feeling of inferiority, the feeling that the others had to do it all while I did little or nothing. Life assumed a happy routine. It was all new and interesting and there was a great deal to learn. I was not sufficiently used to night flying to worry much about the prospects of interception (though there was generally a good deal of gloom about that) but, becoming bit by bit more accustomed to it, I was gaining confidence. I found, contrary to my expectations, that attention to flying instruments could often be relaxed, even on moonless nights—provided I was above all haze and cloud where the stars were bright and a horizon discernible. But getting up there might entail a struggle through thousands of feet of oppressive cloud, the darkness complete, my world confined to the cockpit.

With a half moon or more came a total transformation on a climb through cloud. The darkness would lift as I approached the moonlight and soon the aircraft seemed to bound into clear air, skimming the cloud tops momentarily, and quickly climbing above them into a new world, pale lit, mysterious and beautiful. Above was a dark blue-black sky which here and there was a paler blue, and below was the cloud through whose depths I had been feeling a way a few minutes before, now gentle and harmless looking, a cotton-wool carpet. Up there it was almost like flying in daylight. The patrol over, I would leave the splendour of the night sky with relief, but with regret too, for its beauty never palled. As the aircraft plunged into the cloud like a city-bound tube train into its tunnel, the dark seemed more oppressive than before, and there was nothing but the blind-flying instruments to guide me until, on dead reckoning, the airfield should have been close and my height a few thousand feet. Then and not before did I look up and out.

It might be easy and the aerodrome lights or landmark beacons might be visible at once, but sometimes, with visibility bad, the dim lights of the flare-path (consisting then of aptly styled Glim lamps) and the red lamp on the floodlight tender might be missed altogether or not seen till too late, and then I would have to try again. Going over and back, being given homing bearings, going lower and lower each time to be sure of being out of cloud, trying to get a word in while everyone else in the same predicament as myself was asking for bearings—these were the difficulties, when there were difficulties, in 1940. Night flying was to become much easier.

To find that I could cope with this flying, learning something new each time and increasing my confidence, was satisfying. I could not ask for more just then.

Every other night we would be on the operational programme, to be in a state of readiness to fly from half an hour before sunset until daylight. As the night drew on and enemy activity died down, the first few crews were kept at 'readiness', the others relaxing to 'Available' and going to the mess to sleep, probably undisturbed. At the dispersal point there was a beastly little hut in which we waited while at 'readiness'. It was lit by oil-lamps and later by a single unreliable electric-lamp; it had an oil-stove, which always smelt and often smoked. There were beds, and on these the crews would sprawl, wearing a great amount of clothes, for the heating in our Blenheims was ineffective and temperatures at operational heights were sometimes as low as minus thirty centigrade. The light was dim; it was impossible to read and most of us were not inclined even to try. Early on the talk would range over the war, aircraft, the unpleasantness of night flying, the futility of night fighting and what the last crew down had seen. In the later stages of the night quiet would reign and those who were able to would doze. The telephone would go often, sometimes to pass orders for another patrol and sometimes to give weather reports and other things. Each time it rang it would give me a jab and make me wide awake, particularly if I was next to fly; and if it gave orders for a patrol, I would receive them almost with relief.

As night fighters we were wholly ineffective. We could not find the enemy aircraft, and even had we been able to, our Blenheims, though improved now by the removal of their turrets, were too slow to overhaul them. The radar was unreliable and the operators too inexperienced to use it. It took two to make a successful interception, and at that time some of the pilots could not contribute their share. Our aircraft were hard to keep serviceable, and sometimes we would fly them to a standstill.

One such night when the enemy had been bombing some luckless Midlands city I shall long remember. The weather was fine and it was 3 a.m. We had all flown and now not one of our Blenheims remained fit for operations. Activity had died down an hour or two earlier, and all of us, the air and ground crews, were stretched out on beds in the hut. It was dark and all was still. Most were sleeping.

I was getting drowsy when I heard a familiar, un-synchronised drone; it must have been the last of the night's raiders, and it came, so it seemed, right over-head. Suddenly there were two shattering explosions; the bombs were close. Many of those in the hut may have been woken up, but no one uttered a word except one cockney airman. Using with emphasis a well-worn and all-too-usual expletive, he ejaculated but two words: "Effing sorce!" There was, I thought, in his voice chiefly concern that it was a beastly foreigner, a German at that, who had had the impertinence to wake him so rudely.

Chapter 5

THE FIRST BEAUFIGHTERS

ONE day at the end of October 1940 the first Beaufighter arrived at Middle Wallop. On the ground
it was an ominous and rather unwieldy looking aircraft, with its outsize undercarriage and propellers
and small wings, but in the air it looked just right.

There is never a new machine introduced but some
people whisper that it is dangerous to fly, that its speed
is disappointing and that it is, in general, a wash-out.
Of such criticisms the Beaufighter had more than its
fair share. The reports, however, from those few of
the Squadron who first flew it were favourable. It obviously had a good take-off and it was said to be man-
œuvrable and fast, doing well over 300 miles per hour
at about 15,000 feet. It had tankage for five hours'
patrolling, an improved type of radar, and four cannon.
Most important of all, it had a cockpit out of which
the pilot could see well. First impressions were favourable; but having just become accustomed to the Blenheim, I could not help feeling a bit depressed because
I knew I would have to start again from scratch.

Results and operational experience were urgently
needed, and the first Beaufighter was pressed into
operations immediately, the only pilots to whom it
was entrusted being Mike Anderson and John Cunningham.[1]

[1] Group Captain Cunningham, D.S.O., O.B.E., D.F.C.

The Bristol Aeroplane Co., Ltd.

'On the ground it was an ominous and rather unwieldy-looking aircraft.'

The Beaufighter Mark I equipped with A.I. Mark IV.

Imperial War Museum

' It had a cockpit out of which the pilot could see well . . .'

The Bristol Aeroplane Co., Ltd.

A Beaufighter cockpit

THE FIRST BEAUFIGHTERS

Ignorant of the theoretical side of night interception and inexperienced on the practical side, I was
then sceptical about its prospects. I did not believe it
possible with Blenheims, quite apart from their inadequate speed and radar, and so I doubted whether
Beaufighters would be any more successful. This was a
doubt based only on a 'hunch' of the most reactionary
sort. I had already chased many aircraft and sometimes I had been told that I should be fairly near them,
but I had not yet seen another aircraft in flight at
night and I could not imagine a technique for interception and attack. My discouragement grew, and
sometimes a fleeting and irrational doubt appeared,
the fruit perhaps of a primitive instinct: seeing is
believing and I was not seeing. And later it always
seemed somehow incredible when, after a drawn-out
and exacting chase wholly dependent on electric sight,
a silhouette suddenly took shape, looming up like a
lamp-post in a fog.

The news less than a month after the arrival of the
first Beaufighter that John had destroyed a Junkers 88
was electrifying. For me it meant that the bombers we
were sent to chase were really there and that the cover
of the dark was not absolute. Had further confirmation been needed, it was supplied by Mike, who
destroyed a Heinkel 111 a few nights later. There
seemed something unreal about these combats. To
leave a comfortable Hampshire airfield and to come
upon an intruder over one's own country in the dark,
to shoot at it and watch it go down like a catherine
wheel and explode on hitting the ground, to break the
spell and feel that the cover of darkness was no longer

complete—these were strange and exciting adventures. While John with typical resourcefulness had enabled his observer, Phillipson,[1] to get the contact by investigating a searchlight concentration, Mike had been guided all the way by a ground controller who, with radar, kept track both of the enemy and the Beaufighter, remotely manœuvring the latter to a position from which its own radar could see the enemy and from where Cannon,[2] his observer, could take over. Thus radar had played a key part in both successes, and it was stimulating for some of us to think that the latter interception took place entirely in the dark and under close ground control. Perhaps there was hope yet for the less resourceful; perhaps all of us might see some action before long—such was one line of reasoning.

But contacts alone were useless. Their size and their movement had to be interpreted by the observer and a running commentary maintained to the pilot to give him a picture of what he could not see and had to imagine, and every now and again a quick instruction had to be inserted like 'slow down', 'faster', 'climb a little', 'down a bit' or 'steady, hold it there'. This and the flying of the aircraft made the teamwork which would bring the Beaufighter to a position from which the pilot could see with his own eyes; then it was all up to him, and the four 20-millimetre cannon he controlled. It sounded straightforward; yet I, for one, was still dubious. I doubted my ability to achieve the

[1] Warrant Officer J. R. Phillipson, D.F.C., killed on active service, January 5th, 1943.
[2] Warrant Officer B. Cannon, D.F.M.

high standard of flying which seemed vital to this sort of blind-man's buff, this groping for the enemy. To fly in the dark and at the same time to search for the visual contact by a systematic concentration on the sky seemed a very far-off feat to one who had only just begun to realise that concentration on instruments need not, in some conditions, be incessant. It was plain that we all needed much training and practice; how we were to get it was less obvious.

Radar control from the ground had been on trial in our sector for some months, and many of us had had experience of it in practices, taking the part alternately of the bomber and the fighter. These early experiments were not encouraging, but they had about them an air of scientific investigation that made them interesting for us, although we knew little about the gear used, which then was 'top secret' and was referred to simply as G.C.I. There was an academic ring about the instructions given by the scientist designers (who were then the controllers) to the pilot who, miles high above the sleeping land, was charging about blindfold and trusting. It seemed that the thanks proffered over the radio at the end of a practice or a patrol were appropriate to the completion of a valuable but inconclusive laboratory experiment. But inconclusive though it consistently was so far as I was concerned, G.C.I. was now no longer experimental. We had proof that G.C.I. could direct a radar fighter near enough to an enemy bomber for a contact, and we knew that the Beaufighter had the speed to overhaul it.

The problems facing the higher command must at this time have been exceedingly grave. The enemy were flying over us at night with all but immunity from interception, and our cities were being systematically destroyed. To deal with the night bomber there were plans in profusion; more anti-aircraft guns, more searchlights, more radar fighters, more cat's-eye fighters and more special devices; but with successes so few and experience so slender, there can have been no certainty that priorities were being rightly allocated, and there must have been much relief that there was now a clear indication. A new radar fighter had succeeded in one sector with both ground control and searchlights, and informed circles were probably now optimistic. The pioneering efforts of Mike and John and their observers, and their rewards, were probably as far reaching in their effect on policy as they were laudable in their execution.

We, the aircrew, were happily unconscious of the bigger issues, and our only anxieties outside our own flying task were such seemingly vital domesticities as the establishing of the right to late breakfast, the night-flier's extra egg, or petrol for leave. The activities of the Squadron were really all that mattered in the war, and they were all engrossing. Nevertheless, we could see the proportions of the task in our own sector and it was enormous. It was, in fact, only a small part of that confronting Fighter Command.

Controllers, radar operators and pilots had to be trained in the use of new equipment and in new techniques. When John scored the first success there were but three pilots fit to fly the Beaufighter at night and the same number of competent operators. Method had to be worked out between pilots and their observers and pilots and ground controllers. Each separate operation had to be practised, and then dress rehearsals were needed. Yet the urgency of operations virtually ruled out practice at night because all available aircraft were required for the programme. We all needed practice, but when could we get it? Which comes first, training or operations, the chicken or the egg? This perpetual quandary, which must always beset the high commands in modern war, was very acute just then.

We were up against poor serviceability of new equipment, and ignorance. The Beaufighters had their teething troubles which, though mostly minor, could become serious in night flying. The radar was new and delicate; it broke down frequently; and the mechanics who knew much about it were few. Our radar officers never spared themselves, working, it seemed, day and night, and often flying on operations as well as in tests and practices. The observers had had only the scantiest training, a number of them having been airgunners who had been given a short conversion course. As soon as a pilot was considered fit, he and his observer became operational as a crew. Thereafter they had to practise on the Germans. I shall remember it always by a not unusual incident during a daylight test flight in a Blenheim. I flew some distance behind another aircraft and I told my observer to turn on the radar. There was an "O.K.", a silence and suddenly, a little later, an excited cry "I can see it!", and then, after a few moments of suspense, "It's gone!", and further silence. And that was more than usually occurred, since on most occasions there was nothing to be seen on the radar tubes at all.

By the end of 1940 we had been completely re-equipped, and sufficient pilots, six in all, had been scraped together to allow the operational programme to proceed exclusively with Beaufighters. The Blenheim had disappeared from night fighting so far as we were concerned, and those like myself who had not had the opportunity of flying a Beaufighter at night became non-operational. With impatience we waited for an opportunity for Beaufighter night solos, the essential prelude to becoming operational again; we were short of aircraft and at this season the weather was often bad, and so it was that Mike, John, Georgie,[1] Spekie,[2] Alastair[3] and Jackson[4] were on operations every night for about a month.

After weeks of depressing inactivity, I was given a chance. With low, broken cloud and a forecast of deterioration, the weather was not ideal, but I was no longer a novice and, needing time only for one or two take-offs, circuits and landings, I was let go. What followed was not all my fault, nor can it be attributed wholly to the weather, for soon after I had taken off the control went off the air and all calls were ignored, with the result that I and the three others also airborne assumed the radio, either ground or air, to have failed. There was dangerous confusion. In that weather

[1] Wing Commander G. O. Budd, D.F.C.
[2] Flight Lieutenant H. Speke, D.F.C., killed on active service, July 26th, 1941.
[3] Flight Lieutenant A. S. Hunter, killed on active service, February 6th, 1941.
[4] Pilot Officer P. F. Jackson, D.F.M., killed on active service, May 29th, 1941.

the decision to land while we knew we were near base was inevitable. It was every man for himself and, with the cloud at about 1,000 feet, we came in and landed as we could. I broke cloud, saw the aerodrome lights and, making an ill-judged and hurried approach, came straight in. I was too high and, to make matters worse, I held off too early and opened up a little to reduce the bump. The aircraft touched down and ran on with all the momentum of ten tons moving at eighty miles per hour. I braked hard, but we were on wet grass—there were no runways then and the flare-path, laid out into the wind, was sometimes too short to cover faults—and the boundary lights of the Andover–Salisbury road seemed to be approaching alarmingly. A moment later I was in the road and at rest at last. Suddenly everything was still. I got out and walked away from what had been a perfectly good Beaufighter, feeling rather an ass.

A few nights later I tried again and, all going well, we were reinstated on the operational programme, so that one of the original six crews could then have one night off in six.

With experience my confidence grew. I felt I was becoming accustomed to the Beaufighter and its idiosyncrasies. It was then unstable fore and aft, and so was not ideal for night flying. It always seemed—and this was in the imagination of an anxious mind—that the darker the night the worse was the effect of this instability. If there were sufficient external guides, lights in good visibility, a skyline or moonlit ground, it was easy enough to fly steadily, as in daylight; but if those aids were absent, the night dark and visibility poor, the instruments were the only guides, and instrument flying in the early Beaufighter called for unceasing and most exacting concentration. There were times when the loss or gain of a few hundred feet in the gentle undulation of its normal trajectory could not be afforded, and at such times there had to be no relaxing.

In bad weather a return to base and landing became something of an ordeal. Effective blind approach and airfield lighting systems were yet to come, and at the end of 1940 we had to find our own way as best we could, depending on homing bearings and on recognition of the dim flare-path lights when we were near the airfield.

Condensation and frost, which formed on both sides of the one-and-a-half-inch-thick windscreen as one came down into warmer air, were further impediments and, since the windscreen was close to one's face, there was nothing to do but peer ahead through the small windows on either side of it.

The Beaufighter tended to tighten up in turns, and this, accentuating the ever-present difficulty of making accurate turns on instruments, resulted—at least in my experience—in unwitting gains or losses in height in all but gentle turns. Being usually frightened and so cautious, I made a practice of very gentle turns at low altitude, imagining the consequences of losing too much height, and knowing only too well the embarrassment of blundering back into cloud again by gaining it. The airfield might come into view too late, and going obliquely across the flare-path, unable to make the steep turn that might have got me in, I would have to go on in a wide sweep into the outer darkness again and away from those feeble but homely lights, hoping that when I saw them again I would be better aligned for landing. I would see some lights, but from low altitude their pattern was not plain. Suddenly they became the flare-path, not exactly where I had expected it but off to one side; still I might be able to 'make' it. Perhaps in the act of putting the wheels down hurriedly I would let the machine gain some height. The airfield lights seemed to go out. My immediate instinct was to push the nose down, to lose height and to regain contact with the ground and the guidance of the lights quickly, but my caution made me lose height gingerly; it might yet be all right when, out of cloud, I saw the lights again, or it might not, and then the whole anxious process might have to be repeated.

Finding base and getting down to Mother Earth could be both long and anxious. It seemed that there were no rules to learn, and sometimes when I landed I found myself in a cold sweat, knowing that I had been lucky and wondering what would happen next time.

The acme of unpleasantness was reached one night when the enemy made a serious mistake about the weather and lost five aircraft, probably through icing: a loss which the Press attributed incorrectly but perhaps intentionally to our fighters. The blitz was on Southampton and we were making a maximum effort. The weather was awful. As a new experience for me, there was an icy, electric haze in which I was still floundering at 22,000 feet, unable to reach the clear air. There was a constant bluish discharge from one side of the windscreen to the other and on the airscrew blades, and a ghostly light in the cockpit which made it impossible to see anything outside.

Dependent only on the blind-flying instruments and their dazzling, sickly green needles, I began to feel, as I grew tired, that my power over the machine was becoming uncertain and that I might suddenly find myself unable to control it. My senses denoted turns; yet the needles showed straight flight. I tried to turn left and, depending on my senses (other than my vision), operated the stick and rudder to produce a left turn; but the instruments insisted that I was not turning, and a vicious pull on the controls to produce a turn which the needles would admit caused such sensations that I dared not continue it. But a turn to the right could be made, I found, according to the needles and the pressure on my seat, and so I turned right handed, the long way round. Chasing the enemy was a hopeless proposition. In these conditions it was all I could do to keep myself poised, somewhat unsurely, with my machine more or less under control. My only chance of destroying an enemy in that sort of weather (and, I then thought, in any sort of weather for that matter) was haphazard collision.

As I was feeling my way back to base, a load of incendiaries was dropped just behind me. I was at a few hundred feet only and the glare from them, as they burnt, was reflected in and diffused by the haze in which I was flying in a way that was distracting and, until I guessed its source, alarming. There was a good deal of tight-rope walking that night.

As I have said, we had few opportunities for training at night because all serviceable aircraft were usually required for operations, but on one memorable occasion absence of enemy activity coincided with good local weather and we were able to carry out some interception practice. Groping about in the dark at close on three hundred miles an hour called for steady flying and a cold-blooded nervelessness that I had not got. I had always had vague doubts about it: now I would see what it was like.

Using navigation lights, we took off in pairs, one behind the other, and set off. When all was ready the crew in front extinguished lights and the crew behind tried to approach on radar to within visual range. Instead of the daylight swoop to attack, there had to be a steady and deliberate stalk to close range, then a search, the pilot looking where his observer told him for a small patch that was darker than its surroundings; and finally a stealthy closing up to point-blank range. This much I knew; but how to put theory into practice was another matter, and the machine behind —when it was mine—wandered and weaved about, trying to close in and just maintaining radar contact, sheering off or shooting underneath as the target suddenly loomed up as it were out of a fog, converging frighteningly. After this, my first practice, I was despondent; I felt out of my depth.

At that time, I think, most of us were ignorant as well as inexperienced. We had yet to understand the full significance of the illumination of the background and the size of the silhouette to appreciate that, against bright starlight, a Beaufighter could be seen from a thousand feet below, while against the ground it remained invisible down to about 300 feet. We had not yet learnt that the correct technique was to search (exploiting the fact that our sight is more acute on the periphery than at the centre of the eye) with speeds synchronised so as to avoid blundering on when the invisible opponent, though left behind, would still appear as radar 'blips', seeming (until the observers too had acquired experience) to be drawing away ahead. We did not yet possess the encouraging knowledge that most aircraft, except our Beaufighters, had telltale exhausts, and that surprise could always be on the side of the radar fighter against a bomber without radar. There was much we had to discover and develop for ourselves, for it was new ground we were breaking.

That winter (1940) there was a short spell of brilliantly clear and very cold nights, and the enemy took full advantage of them, keeping up his raids, it seemed to us, all night long. We did all we could, flying long patrols on several consecutive nights, but it was of no avail. Six crews reported about seventy radar contacts, but all were lost inconclusively. In our contribution of thirteen hours' patrolling during those three nights, my observer and I got and lost our first contact on an enemy aircraft.

It seemed to me that our efforts had reached a crisis, and while I had the small satisfaction of knowing that I was not alone in being unsuccessful, I was concerned about my own part in it. I was tired, having had no adequate leave for what seemed many months—the crew shortage allowed us only to snatch a day or two here and there—and I had sore eyes, caused by prolonged exposure to draught (it came up through the crack between the escape hatch and the fuselage side; it curled up over your head and caught you straight in the eyes) and my confidence had recently been badly shaken by some unnerving returns and landings of the sort I have already tried to describe. I was beginning to think that I would not be able to pull it off the next time and that I would fall off the tight-rope; and in that low state of mind I was relieved to be sent away for a fortnight's course on beam flying and blind approach.

This gave me a welcome change from night flying, and incidentally allowed my eyes to recover. I learnt a way of approaching, unseeing, to land at an airfield by using a beam transmitted from that airfield as a guide. It would be possible, in any weather, to approach from a distance with deliberation, and the certainty that, on breaking cloud, one would be correctly placed to land straight ahead. Thus the tempo of the operation would be slowed down and it would become more manageable.

The operation (hitherto hit-and-miss so far as I was concerned) of finding and landing at an airfield in bad weather could now be done by following rules, and then safe arrivals, which had been accidental and so destructive of confidence, would now, if achieved by following the rules, have just the opposite effect. I returned from the course with new confidence and feeling well and refreshed.

Chapter 6

PITFALLS AND PATROLS

LATE one night after flying, as I was walking back to the mess, I saw a bright flash in the direction of Andover. It lit up the sky, and immediately afterwards I was hearing the tearing scream of racing engines. Then all seemed still. This, I realised, had been an aircraft falling out of control and crashing some miles away. It seemed strange that the crew, unless they had got out, must have been dead while I was still hearing those engines. Although I never heard what had happened, I do not doubt that, like many other night-flying accidents, this one also remained a complete mystery. For good reason I was inquisitive and, as an exercise, I used to try to imagine for myself how these accidents happened, for, when I thought I knew, I regained that important belief: 'it will never happen to me'.

I have mentioned the misleading sensations to which, I believe, most pilots are subject when they are tired and flying on instruments; how one can feel a turn yet not be turning, or find oneself apparently incapable of turning in one direction, though able to turn in the other. These deceptions by one's sensations—for they are deceptions; the instruments are right—are harmless if they are recognised as deceptions and ignored, but sometimes when things happen suddenly and the sensations are acute—in a spin or a spiral off a stall or a diving turn—they cannot be ignored, and instinct, reacting to them, may assert itself ruinously. Then the pilot, no better than a drowning man, may not be able to reassert reason over instinct—and probably there is no time for recovery.

Sheer fright and the lack of lights taught me, when I started, the first rule for taking-off in the dark: go on to instruments as soon as possible and avoid looking out until several hundred feet up. What could happen if this rule was not observed was suggested by several otherwise inexplicable crashes of single-seaters at take-off, accidents in clear weather, in which the machine dived to the ground after a normal take-off. In the light of an everyday parallel of which I read in a medical journal when I was a staff officer several months later, and which was subsequently used in training, these strangely recurrent accidents, so mysterious in their origin, acquired a likely explanation, and with their mystery they lost all their menace.

The pilot taking off is like a man standing in a tube train. The train accelerates leaving the station, and in the tunnel the lights fail. To counteract the acceleration the traveller leans forward instinctively, and this he continues to do in the dark tunnel. Were he asked what impression he had in the tunnel when the lights were out, he would probably say that he thought the train had been going uphill, and he would have the firm belief that he had been standing upright and not leaning forward. In fact, the train was going downhill, as is usual for a tube train when it leaves a station.

The parallel between the pilot taking off and the man in the tube train is close. The aircraft moves off, accelerating quickly, and the lights, which from those single-seaters could only be seen as they flashed by, become less intelligible. It becomes airborne, climbing and still accelerating; and now all is strange. Looking out, the pilot can no longer see any lights. There are no external guides and the oblique visibility near the ground is, as usual, poor; even the stars are dim and there is no horizon; the only guide is the pressure on his seat. His situation has become like that of the man in the darkened train. His sensations may satisfy him that he is climbing, but they have deceived him; he is not climbing—he may even have thought he was climbing too steeply and pushed the stick forward—and at that low altitude split seconds count. He may realise his mistake, but it will be too late.

This was helpful to me and probably to others. The absolute need for instrument flying was evident and the reason why was understood. The many night-flying accidents attributed to errors of judgment were no longer the mysteries they had been, and it seemed that I had learnt this lesson without having to have the experience; but much to my shame I later gave myself an expensive and convincing demonstration, which taught me the lesson once more at the price of another damaged Beaufighter.

There was a full moon and one might have described it, inaccurately, as almost as light as day. I was ordered off and I taxied out. As usual, I had my seat well raised for taxi-ing and, being taken in by the brilliance of the moonlight, I did not lower it when I was ready to go. I took off as in daylight, looking not at the instruments but out and ahead. I was conscious of a moment of uneasiness just as I became airborne and automatically I looked down at the instruments and climbed away steadily, but not before I had bounced back on to the ground again with a severe bump. Some hours later, still remembering that bump, I came back to land, and I found that the undercarriage would not lock down. I flew around for some time, trying everything I knew without success, and came in hoping that it was only the indicators that were at fault. But it was not; the undercarriage collapsed soon after I touched down.

This accident was inexcusable, but it was interesting too. Its cause might have remained a mystery had I not admitted an error of judgment, and stated in my report that the damage had probably been done at take-off. My honesty earned for me a well-deserved 'rocket' from Group.

In December 1940 John destroyed two Heinkels at dusk over the Channel. Seemingly contemptuous or ignorant of the existence of our fighter defence, the enemy was then starting early, the pathfinders crossing the Channel at last light. Consequently our fighters had to be out well before sunset, and the first two machines would go off from Middle Wallop when the daylight was beginning to fade.

Flying south at that time of day was impressive. More often than not one soon regained the sunlight, leaving below the usual haze and murk of twilight. This was just the time when, in my earlier service with the Squadron, I might have been landing, relieved that I was getting down while it was yet light, for we had no radio then and navigation depended on ability to see. To go up above the haze or cloud at dusk, losing all coherent sight of the ground, would then have been rash; and to me, subject to an inborn instinct and still liking to be independent of radio (navigation by which I accepted as a necessary evil associated with the dark), going out on a dusk patrol always remained preoccupying, for it was not yet dark and I was not yet resigned to being led like a blind man. Yet radio, I knew, would help me back, and I found this new power, which let me defy these timid qualms, exciting. All the same, my enjoyment of the indescribable beauty and tranquillity of my surroundings was a little marred by more than normal uneasiness over the prospect of returning to earth.

When we reached the coast we would go out towards Cherbourg at 10,000 to 12,000 feet, and in mid-Channel one machine would turn east and the other west to take up their patrol beats. The scene was superb. The sun came down, huge, to the horizon and imperceptibly sank below it. The light withdrew gracefully and, it seemed, reluctantly from the western sky. It was great fortune to be a regular witness of these scenes, which people would climb mountains to see and then would see only once; and how strange it was to be doing this celestial sight-seeing in a crude, noisy flying machine pulled by about three thousand horse-power and full of complex equipment; and how grotesque it was that all this effort was aimed at bringing guns within range of another flying machine carrying a load of bombs intended for a city in my country.

So the musings went on and the time passed. It became quite dark. The stars came out and blue-blackness became uniform from east to west. Now, decently cloaked by the dark, I felt more secure. Cherbourg and the Channel Isles, which had looked uncomfortably close, were now invisible, and gone and forgotten was my anxiety over finding base again. With the dark came acceptance of the radio and some modest self-assurance. Patrolling at night was no longer the ordeal it used to be. The anxious and far too frequent round of inspection of engine instruments, the endless fiddling with the flimsy bits of paper which gave the key to the flashing beacons, and the general tension were, I began to think, memories. My world had opened out from the confines of a cockpit to the vastness of the night sky from horizon to horizon. I had learnt to relax and to fly straight and level by the stars, holding them stationary, a group tucked up in the corner of the windshield; and the north star had become familiar. I had found that provided the air was clear I could take liberties, turning hard to make the sudden course corrections that might save an otherwise vanishing contact. I remembered well my first patrol. I was wound up like a spring, and I could not relax; it was very exhausting. Now, it seemed, I had found the secret, and in this element I was becoming proficient —or I thought I was, until I had to return to land. Then, going down through cloud, most of my assurance evaporated and I understood again the feelings I had when I started; and I knew that every approach and landing in difficult weather was still an adventure for me. I had thought of it as tight-rope walking, and then I learnt to use the beam. When that worked it became perhaps more like crossing a stream by a high, single-plank bridge with no hand-rail; it was just like that: to keep your feet dry keep on the plank, but to do this you had to keep your head.

As time went on, the flying became mechanical. Two seven zero, then zero nine zero, backwards and forwards this sentry-go went on and on. Sometimes there might be a fruitless chase after a bomber whose presence seemed vaguely improbable, and then back to the beat. There were probably few distractions, and my thoughts, like those of one troubled with sleeplessness, would range far and wide; sometimes the even rhythm of the engines suggested music which would fill my head and help to pass the time; but usually the patrol went on too long and all my resources became exhausted. I would become bored, and would find myself looking at my watch every few minutes, longing for my release.

It was usually three hours before the welcome order came 'return to base and pancake'; and although the patrol had probably been monotonous and uneventful, and although I was resigned by now to night-fighter patrols until the end of the war, with the dejected belief that others might, but I would not, succeed, nevertheless after a spell like this I had at least the satisfaction of feeling tired, thinking that I had done all I could.

Enemy action hardly touched us, and it was usually accident which stole from amongst us men with whom we were sharing the excitement, trials and tribulations of our task and whom we had got to know and to like,

66

such men as Alastair Hunter, Spekie, Nigel,[1] Jackson
and others. It was Alastair who had scored the Squadron's first victory soon after the fall of France by destroying a float-plane over the Channel, and he was
one of our most experienced pilots. He was gay, happy
and confident, and he seemed to take flying in his stride.
He and Genny,[2] his observer, were badly missed; the
accident, like so many others, was unaccountable.

The night it happened I was on operations, but I
did not fly, having to miss my turn because my aircraft was not ready. A Beaufighter with, among other
things, a much-improved windscreen, had been sent to
Middle Wallop for trials, and it was offered to me
that evening to test while I waited; but it was strange
to me and I demurred, going instead to the mess for
supper. We talked at supper of the modified Beaufighter, and Alastair, though off-duty, volunteered to
fly it, adding that he had nothing better to do. Genny,
a veteran with an M.C. from the first war, went with
him. They were already in the air when I got back to
the wretched little bungalow at the far end of the airfield which served as our dispersal point, and there I
waited at 'readiness', my aircraft being by then serviceable.

Suddenly I heard an excited voice outside: "Mr.
Hunter has crashed." I went outside: "Where,
where?" "Not sure, sir," and "They say he was coming in to land," and I thought: "That will be all right.

---

[1] Flying Officer N. R. Wheatcroft, killed on active service,
November 26th, 1940.

[2] Pilot Officer T. Genny, M.C., killed on active service,
February 6th, 1941.

He has probably undershot and landed short, breaking the undercarriage." It had happened before, that sort of thing.

I was joined by Stanley Skinner,[1] and I gave him the news; he also was not unduly worried. It never entered our heads that Alastair could have met with a serious accident; he was a very capable pilot and he had done hundreds of hours at night. We waited, Stanley and I, telephoning now and again to the operations-room to ask for news; but they had none and none seemed forthcoming. It was only known that there had been a crash somewhere off the aerodrome in the down-wind direction, which was on the opposite side to our dispersal area.

We decided to go over and see for ourselves. I think the idea we both had was that we might be able to cheer the crew up if they had been hurt; but the thought that they *had* been hurt had hardly entered my head. We trudged across the aerodrome to the beginning of the flare-path, and there we talked to the control officer. It was he who had seen the crash and reported it. "Oh no. It was some distance away. I saw the lights go down. It seemed as if he was turning." So it was not just a landing accident. Still, there had been no fire. Perhaps the motors had cut and he had had to make a wheels-up landing.

We walked on in the direction he had shown us, still thinking that all must be well, yet hoping and hoping that all was in fact well. We went on outside

[1] Wing Commander S. H. Skinner, killed August 19th, 1942, while acting as observer with naval forces during the Dieppe raid.

the aerodrome boundary; we plodded on across heavy ploughed land. The mud stuck to my flying-boots and, still in my voluminous flying-clothes, I began to sweat with the exertion. We talked about the crash as we trudged, and we discussed how it could have happened. The idea was fixed in my mind that the crew was safe, and I almost expected to meet them walking in; I believed firmly that the miracle which sometimes happened had happened once more. I was able to ignore the fact that a Beaufighter would hit the ground at the speed of an express train.

We saw lights ahead and we went towards them. We passed a large shape, and I saw that it was a petrol tank. It was well ahead of the rest of the machine where the lights were. I knew what this meant and my heart sank. This was no ordinary forced landing; this was a serious crash. We approached the lights, and we saw that some lorries, probably the fire-tender and the ambulance, were there playing their headlights on the scene. We drew nearer and saw a semicircle of men facing the wreck with their backs to us. As I came up close I saw between two of those people, in the glare of the headlights, a mass of wreckage, and across and over it there sprawled helplessly a leg in a flying-boot. This glimpse told me the whole story, and I drew back into the darkness, murmuring mechanically to one of the men in the semicircle who, I suppose, had helped to pull them out: "Are they dead?" I knew what the answer was going to be. He said: "Yes. Both dead." I walked away into the darkness by myself, feeling a bit dizzy and trying to say a prayer.

We walked back to the mess. There was nothing we

could do out there. We talked for the sake of talking, mechanically, about how it could have happened. We showed no emotion; we were not very conscious of what we were saying; we had to talk.

No one could ever know for certain how this accident had come about, and it was put down, as so many night-flying accidents had to be, to an error of judgment, an error that any one of us might have made.

CHAPTER OF DARKNESS

Chapter 7

SUCCESS AND TRIBULATION

ON the night of March 13th, 1941, the unexpected happened. I destroyed two enemy aircraft. This was luck unbounded, and these were experiences which I knew could never be equalled. For the rest of that night it was impossible to sleep; there was nothing else I could talk about for days after; there was nothing else I could think about for weeks after.

With these victories—and even one of them would have sufficed—a great deal had suddenly become worth while, and this was success such as I had never dreamt of; it was sweet and very intoxicating. I saw my name in the papers, and the Squadron, so long in obscurity, coming into the limelight; for these were its sixth and seventh confirmed successes. It became suddenly 'a famous night-fighter squadron'. The public was let into the secret; it was equipped with Beaufighters and there were veiled allusions to a secret weapon. There was a lot of glamour and excitement attached to being a night-fighter pilot; we felt a good deal beyond ourselves.

On that night there was an almost full moon and the weather was very fine. We had been flying for more than an hour when we were put on to a bomber that was going back empty. We were overtaking fairly well, and by the time we passed over Bournemouth were about a mile behind. We closed in a bit more and Ripley, my observer, got a close radar contact over to the left. I turned a little to the left, and I could hardly believe my eyes, for there was another aircraft about a hundred yards away and on the same level. It was black and its fish-like fuselage glistened dully in the moonlight; it was unmistakably a Heinkel.

Converging rapidly, I turned to come behind and dropped below with an automatism that surprised me; my machine seemed to be on rails, so easily did it slide into position. I was afraid I would be seen in that light—and the Beaufighter would have been a sitter—but interceptions were not expected then, and the enemy gunners were not keeping a good look-out. I was able to creep up unmolested until I was within a hundred yards and forty-five degrees below. The machine looked enormous; the wings seemed to blot out the sky above me; now, a squat silhouette, it had lost its recognisable form. I saw the four rows of exhausts, each with six stubs, and now and again one of them would belch out a bigger flame than usual.

The moment had come to shoot; it was now or never. Holding my breath I eased the stick back a little and the Heinkel came down the windscreen and into the sight. It went too far and I found myself aiming above. Stick forward a bit and the sight came on it again. How ham-fisted this was! I pressed the firing-button. There was a terrific shaking and banging, and to my surprise I saw flashes appearing, as it seemed, miraculously on the shape in front of me. Pieces broke away and came back at me. I kept on firing, and it turned away to the right slowly, apparently helplessly and obviously badly damaged. My ammunition finished I drew away farther to the right. I had overshot, and I could see the Heinkel over my left shoulder still flying all right. Nothing happened, perhaps nothing was going to happen, and suddenly I thought that it was going to get away. I had had a chance, a sitter, and I had not hit it hard enough. It seemed that I had succeeded in the almost impossible feat of firing two hundred 20-millimetre shells at this aircraft at point-blank range without destroying it. It had been like the crazy kitchen side-show at a fair, impossible not to hit something; but here, so I began to think, I had hit nothing vital.

And then I saw a lick of flame coming from the starboard engine. It grew rapidly, and enveloped the whole engine and soon most of the wing. The machine turned east and started to go down slowly; it looked by now like a ball of flame. We followed it down from 11,000 feet until, minutes later, it hit the sea, where it continued to burn.

It was said that the crew baled out, but none was picked up. I did not think of them any more than they probably had thought of the people they had been bombing. This kind of warfare, though in some ways cold-blooded murder, was as impersonal as it was mechanical. This was a big-game hunt, and thought was focused on personal achievement. In the aftermath it was satisfactory to know that the enemy bomber force had been reduced by one, but immediately it was the elation of personal success with neither regrets nor outraged scruples that monopolised my thoughts.

We had one or two more chases which came to

nothing and, having been on patrol for three and a half hours, we went back to land. The aircraft was refuelled and rearmed, and within thirty minutes we were again at 'readiness'. It was about midnight, and although activity usually stopped by midnight, there were on that night still a few enemy bombers going back from the Midlands. We were ordered off.

A chase started soon after take-off; it went on, and I began to despair, for I knew that these bombers without their loads would be going back quickly. After nearly fifteen minutes I was told to turn back north and come home. We were then at about 10,000 feet over the sea, and there was a lane of reflected moonlight on the water stretching south to a small bank of cloud. As I started to turn left towards the north I saw far below a sight which I could hardly believe—the navigation lights of an aircraft flying south. I called up and asked if there were any friendly aircraft about, and the answer came 'No', so I made to follow the lights I had seen. Enemy aircraft had been seen before now flying home brazenly with all lights on; this perhaps was another of them.

I watched the lights intently and started to lose height, trying not to overshoot them. Then they went out and I followed blindly. The thin layer of cloud I had seen to the south intervened, and I reckoned that if the aircraft was skimming along the top, I would have a good chance of seeing it—it was tempting, day or night, to skim along just above the cloud—but I saw nothing. We were now at 5,000 feet and we went down to 4,000, where we were below cloud. As we came out into clear air, Ripley got a contact ahead and close. I started to search and soon, in that light, I saw an aircraft about 2,000 feet away and dead ahead.

I closed in quickly and, recognising it as a Heinkel, dropped below and crept up to sure firing range. Coming up I opened fire from about a hundred and fifty yards. There were flashes on the fuselage and the starboard engine, which lost a cowling and started to emit smoke and sparks. I drew away to await developments, thinking that it would be forced down at once, but instead it started to climb, making for the cloud layer not far above. Hurriedly I opened fire again, but the rear gunner, recovered by now, opened fire and red streaks came past which made me wince and break away to the left.

I followed, climbing well above so that I might see it against the cloud below. Soon I saw that about a mile ahead there was clear air, the cloud ending abruptly. This Heinkel was hard hit and its chances of getting back were, I reckoned, nil; and then I saw ahead—how far I could not judge, but it was perhaps not more than a few miles—a vivid explosion on the sea. We went to the spot and circled, but there was nothing to be seen. I called up to report the combat and find my position, and I was surprised that we were only a few miles south of the Isle of Wight.

We went home to bed, tired after five hours very active flying and blissfully contented. After this successful but wakeful night, I discovered that I had become, according to the more exaggerated Press accounts, a minor 'ace'.

These were brilliant times for us. Successes, once they had started, came fast, and the lessons learnt from each by aircrews and controllers brought more successes. Although the nation's fortunes of war were as low as they had ever been, our particular war was then being loudly acclaimed as a victory of a sort, and that was all that mattered to most of us.

The enemy was sending picked crews ahead of his raids to find the targets and start fires as guides to the bombing force which was following. Late one evening we intercepted one of these pathfinders. There was that groping pursuit, then the sight of twinkling exhausts and the stealthy unseen approach to a position below and close enough for there to be no mistakes. I came up and opened fire, and it was all over very quickly. It was not surprising that the two survivors of the crew did not know what had hit them, for the aircraft exploded, seeming to burst open after the first few rounds, and we were left alone, with the sky to ourselves, the only visible reminder of that aircraft being the oil which smothered our windscreen and forced us to return to base. Well I remember the quiet "Well done" from the station commander, who was waiting on the tarmac. Later that night I destroyed a second Heinkel and two nights later a third. It was characteristic of this sort of warfare that these two nights' flying alternated with attendances at the Sadler's Wells ballet, which was performing at a nearby camp.

I had passed a milestone in my flying by the completion of one hundred hours at night; I had become fairly experienced. This seemed a long way from the timid flying at the training school.

With such successes came a heady self-confidence

and the conviction that interception was not only the best counter-measure to the night bomber, being within the powers of even average crews, but that it should seldom fail. From being incredulous and sceptical I quickly became over-confident, forgetting that moonlight or near twilight (and even navigation lights) and the unawareness of the enemy had allowed me to score. Then my confidence would disappear with a succession of failures, reminders that the real dark multiplied difficulties incredibly, and doubts about the adequacy of my own flying assailed me. It was testing to be close to an opponent, unseen though known to be within visual range, sometimes flying through his slipstream with a sickening bump, and to persevere, waiting for the hail of bullets from an alert gunner (which, in fact, seldom came), with the suspicion growing all the time that the radar was at fault—for this early type could lie most perfectly. Did I fly steadily enough when things were not going well? How did my flying compare with that of others? Their accounts were usually most reticent, and I wondered whether most were more stable or simply less impressionable than I.

With these failures came the suspicion that the enemy, now expecting interception though probably unaware of the approach of individual fighters, was taking routine evasive action: a small turn off course then back being enough to keep the pursuer always at a distance, noticing the turns after they had started and swinging about always on the outside of them.

A dark night when Plymouth was being blitzed for the fourth time in succession was typical of the many occasions when all this was brought disconcertingly home to me. We were sent after an enemy aircraft which was leaving the target and, getting an early contact, we overhauled it steadily. Hopes began to rise and then, as we reached a position from which I might have seen it (but only after a search and knowing which section of the sky to scan), some relative movement started. The enemy slid off quickly to one side, and we had to turn hard to keep the contact. Soon we were weaving about doing hard turns first one way and then the other as if we were on the end of a whip. We lost distance and our oscillations diminished until we were able to settle down to an approach again. Each time we closed in the same thing happened, and finally we were called off and sent after another bomber which was approaching the target. Again all went well until we were a few hundred yards away. We had climbed to 19,000 feet, and I believed that in the glare of the burning city I would not fail to see this aircraft; it should be flying steadily here for its bombing run. But there ensued the same depressing sequence of turns one way and then the other, sometimes becoming hard turns so as to keep the enemy ahead in our radar's field of vision, with never a moment to steady up and endeavour to construe what was happening. And having seen in the inferno far below the flashes of bomb bursts, bombs perhaps dropped by our opponent, we had again to give up. That night the streets of Plymouth stood out, clear dark furrows in the flames. We went home considerably chastened.

Comparing notes the next day with John, I learnt

that he and Jimmie[1] (his air gunner since 1936 and now his radar operator) had chased one aircraft almost to Cherbourg before they had had to give up, and then I felt less dejected.

By May 1941 the Squadron score, which had been mounting steadily, was in the thirties; we led others by a comfortable margin. The system for doing what a year before was almost unheard of was no longer experimental but firmly established. There was no knowing how far the technique would develop before the war ended. It seemed that night was slowly being turned into day. How long, I wondered, would it take for defence to overcome the disadvantage of the dark. How long would it be worth bombing at night? How long would it take us to develop radar to a pitch that would allow us to repulse bombers at night as we had by day? These were interesting speculations.

My luck deserted me. One thing after another went wrong, and sometimes I seemed fated to choose a wrong course when decisions had to be made quickly and there was one right course that might earn the much-needed success. I had a glimpse of an enemy aircraft over Bristol, silhouetted against the glow of fires on the cloud a thousand or so feet below. Perhaps prompt action, a steep dive, would have let me keep it in sight until my observer could pick out the radar contact, but I hesitated and it passed out of sight, screened by one of the engines, and did not reappear. Some nights later my guns jammed when I was behind a Heinkel, close and unseen—this would have

[1] Squadron Leader C. F. Rawnsley, D.S.O., D.F.C., D.F.M.

been a certainty—and having fired a round or two I could do nothing but try to avoid the return fire and save our own skins. On a night in May a deplorable error was saved from having tragic results by what then seemed a miracle.

We were sent down to the coast west of Portland to look for low-flying enemy aircraft which had been reported. It was late and we had already been on patrol for an hour and a half. There was little chance of success, but I hoped and expected that my luck would change; there was a moon and the weather was good. Approaching the coast, I reduced height. It was a beautiful night, and flying south it was easy to see, as we crossed it, the irregular line of demarcation between complete and incomplete blackness which was the coastline. "Vector one eight zero for ten miles and then patrol east and west." The controller had little else to say, and I guessed rightly that not much was known about those low-flying aircraft. It was a wild-goose chase and my confidence evaporated; I was pleased to be soon told to return to base.

Near the coast the radio voice warned me of the presence of another aircraft, saying ominously: "You are being followed by another aircraft. Orbit once." Without any further clue as to the identity of my shadower, I construed that it was the needle in the haystack which, in my optimism, I almost expected to find. I turned the switch that cut off all contact with the outside world so as to have uninterrupted conversation with my observer. We started to search and soon got a contact. After a few changes of course, we were going west and were closing in comfortably. Then I saw a small indistinct shape, barely a silhouette, about 2,000 feet away; for there was a half moon.

We had found to our cost that the enemy were, by then, keeping a good look-out in moonlight; they had been able to get away several times, diving as the fighter closed in or opening fire unexpectedly early. I wanted no mistake this time, and with my eyes glued to this almost shapeless patch of darkness I came in fast, all set to fire as soon as I was satisfied that it was what I expected it to be, hostile. The shape became more distinct; it had all the squatness of the Heinkels I had seen before; there was no doubt in my mind: it was a Heinkel. My approach was not seen, and I was able to close well in before opening fire. I gave a burst and I saw hits on the starboard wing. With another there was a big flash on the port engine; the port wheel came down. It was still flying, but probably, damaged as it was, it would not get home. We had only to follow, reload the guns and finish it off, if it had not already fallen into the sea. The experimental graticule pattern in the gunsight which I was using had done nothing to improve my shooting; it had perhaps made it worse.

I was overtaking all the time, and I overshot, pulling away to the right. The damaged machine turned left towards the sea and across the moon. As the moon caught it I saw something that I would not accept; that tail was familiar. Was it familiar? A thought came to my mind, and I smothered it. It was not possible; it was unthinkable. There was no question that this was not an enemy aircraft; I had been told it was hostile. But had I? One had to make up one's mind in moonlight quickly and from a long way off; otherwise the chance would be lost. And once one's mind was made up there was no drawing back; the rear gunner might shoot first, and his aim would be deliberate. Perhaps it was not a Heinkel; it might be a Junkers 88; I had never seen one of them at night. But there was the shape of that tail, and back came the awful doubt.

All this flashed through my mind, and then I called up, as was the normal procedure, to report that I had had a combat. The answer to my excited message was calm and there were no congratulations. The voice said: "That was probably a friendly aircraft. Follow it and report its position. How badly damaged is it?" I felt as if I had taken an ice-cold plunge. The bottom fell out of my world. I knew now why the tail of that aircraft had looked familiar. The two men inside it were on my side and I had probably killed them; probably they were from my Squadron. John Cunningham and Edward Crew [1] were flying; it might be either of them.

"Why the hell didn't you tell me that it was a 'friendly' which was following me?"

"We could not get in touch with you." Of course they could not get in touch with me when it was too late. Why could they not have warned me at once, when they told me I was being followed? What I had done scarcely bore contemplation.

We followed the crippled aircraft, with one wheel

[1] Wing Commander E. D. Crew, D.S.O., D.F.C.

hanging grotesquely down, for four or five minutes as it turned slowly from south to east and then towards north. And then, against a darker part of the sky, I lost sight of it. That this aircraft was still flying did not mean that the pilot was still alive; damaged aircraft can fly on with no one in control for some time. But there was a little hope. Then on the radio I heard:

"One engine is still working. They hope to make their base." That meant that the pilot was still alive.

"Follow close and report your position if you can."

"I have lost sight of him and I do not know my position."

"The crew is going to bale out. Is it over the sea or land?"

"I do not know."

I was instructed to return to base; there was nothing I could do now. The sight, some minutes later, of a fire on the ground suggested that the machine had crashed on land, and that the crew, had it been possible to bale out, was safe. I reported what I had seen and went home, my mind a seething, unhappy turmoil. I had done a terrible thing. Was it possible, I wondered, that the crew was safe and sound? It would have been a miracle if neither member had been touched.

It seemed to take an age to fly the eighty miles to base. I landed, taxied in, got out and stumbled towards the 'readiness' room. I pushed the door open and went in, blinking and dazzled by the lights. Someone—I forget who it was—was lying on a bed; he was the only chap left there. He said sleepily: "Hullo." I said: "I've shot down a Beau," and he said: "God!

I'm sorry. Bloody bad luck." That, I felt, was decent of him. I would not have been surprised had he said something like "I never want to speak to you again." A stupid idea, but that is how I felt.

I telephoned to Operations and was told what I had realised, that it had been a machine from a squadron in a neighbouring sector. There was no news of the crew, but from the radio conversation it seemed that both members were untouched. A little later I heard that the pilot was safe, and after a further agonising wait came like news about the observer. A load was lifted from me. No longer did I brand myself a fratricide. A mistake had been made; the results were not fatal and that was all that mattered to me just then.

At the enquiry on the next day I met the crew of the machine which I had destroyed, the men whom I had, not so long before, done my best to kill, and I found that I knew the pilot fairly well, having been on a course with him only a few weeks before. Together at this meeting, the strangeness of which we both appreciated, we had an interesting post-mortem on the affair. He asserted that a tip I had given him while we were on that course had let him make good his exit by parachute. We had learnt that of the two escape hatches the pilot's was often difficult to open (there was an automatic release which was not dependable), and it had been made a standard drill that if a crew had to bale out the observer would come forward to help to open the pilot's hatch before going out by his own. In this case it was only by their joint efforts that the pilot's hatch was opened. Despite the poor marksmanship, largely attributable to the experimental gunsight graticule—for the range was very close—the damage done, they said, was heavy. Both engines were hit and one stopped at once; both petrol tanks were holed; the hydraulics were wrecked and, as I had seen, a wheel came down; a few shells had whistled over the pilot's head and gone out just above the windscreen. As often as not an aircraft well hit by cannon shells would blow up. I thought that it was more than luck that had saved that Beaufighter crew.

Some weeks after this baleful episode my luck turned and we intercepted in quick succession two Heinkels heading for the Midlands. In the ensuing combats one was only damaged, but the second blew up after a short burst, like a match being struck, and spun down leaving only a plume of smoke.

Chapter 8

SPEKIE

THE selection of all aircrews, and of pilots in particular, was searching, and at any time between first interview and the completion of the tour of duty the unsuitable might be eliminated. Some who were passed by the doctors were failed by the instructors, and others who had been passed by both came to grief in the squadrons, a very few proving themselves unequal to operations and many others showing a stubborn inability to progress. Expensive accidents in squadrons could ill be afforded, and sometimes it did not need a repetition for a pilot to be transferred to a less demanding rôle. In this way one old member of the Squadron had had to be posted away, for he had crash-landed two Beaufighters in a week, although he had previously mastered the Blenheims well, having once succeeded in force-landing at night without hurt to his observer or himself. He reappeared later as a pilot of Hurricanes protecting convoys, and he explained that this rôle, which involved being catapulted from and probably baling out near a ship, was appropriate because landing had always been his weakness.

But sometimes the benefit of the doubt (when there was a doubt) was given and a career was allowed to continue, and so it was that Spekie, who had been a slow starter in the Squadron, was allowed to remain and became by great perseverance an effective pilot. Spekie was one of those to whom flying came with difficulty, such as most pilots to whom it came naturally cannot gauge, and it was only by superhuman courage and tenacity that he succeeded. He had not made a very good start, and with the war and serious night flying in the blackout, his difficulties assumed new and greater significance. Not many, I think, believed in their innermost thoughts that he would survive for long. Night-flying accidents were all too common in those days; the dark was formidable and a number of pilots, though experienced and steady, had come to grief in it.

Efforts were made to keep him on day flying, but he was not to be deterred. He forged ahead, and eventually persuaded the C.O. to let him go solo one night in a Blenheim; but this ended in disaster. On his approach to land everything seemed to get out of control, and the machine went crashing through some trees into a field a few hundred yards from the aerodrome; the aircraft was completely wrecked and a cow was knocked stone dead. Its death was a bitter blow because its incensed owner broke off the negotiations, initiated by Spekie, for the use by a privileged few of the lavatory in his house, which was near the Squadron dispersal point, the latter then being innocent of such conveniences. Spekie was never allowed to forget this incident.

He was now reckoned to be dangerous, and he was forbidden to fly again at night; but somehow he succeeded in getting another chance, and that time all went well. After that he made steady progress, and by mid-1941 he had flown more hours at night and more consistently in bad weather than any other pilot in the Squadron; but he did not achieve this eminence without some hair-raising adventures, and his survival made one think he had a charmed life. He flew into a balloon cable and it slipped off the end of the wing instead of cutting it off. Lost after a brave and almost hopeless chase with unserviceable radio, he crash-landed a Blenheim at night on a strange aerodrome without lights. On another night he came down in a Beaufighter, from heaven knows what height to a few thousand feet, in what he believed to be a spin (it was an absolutely uncontrolled manœuvre whatever it was) before he could regain control, and proof of the unusualness of the manœuvre was a gaping hole in the side of the cockpit, a window blown clean out. When he came into the hut after landing, he admitted to me that he had thought he was finished: "This is really it. They will all say 'Spekie has done it again.'"

Though one of the first to fly the Beaufighter at night and reckoned as experienced when most of us had done but a few hours, he had no luck, and by early summer, when most of us had destroyed one or two, he had not even had a combat. He was dogged by such consistent bad fortune that he began, in his humility, to think that he lacked something without which success would always remain beyond his grasp. He applied to be transferred to heavy bombers, but his application was turned down flat. He was disappointed, but he hid his disappointment from all but a very few and there was no outward sign of discouragement. He went on trying hard, and his con-

Spekie and John

'. . . it was a point of honour with him to fly
all types of aircraft . . .' Gerald, the Station
Commander, in the unit's Hurricane (*see p.* 117)

'. . . with Charlie Appleton, our new C.O.'
John Cunningham (L), Charles Appleton (R)

gratulations to the lucky ones were always the most
sincere.

Then a plot was hatched—I never knew who was
the originator but always suspected Derek Jackson [1]—
whereby he should fly for a spell with Spekie on the
former's free nights. Derek, a notable scientist, a fear-
less steeplechase rider and a great individualist, was
under training to become a wireless operator/air-
gunner, the job of his choice, when our station commander contrived his posting to the Squadron to help
in raising the standard of radar operating; now he
flew with outstanding success with Charles Appleton, [2]
our new C.O. On the night of May 3rd Derek and
Spekie destroyed an enemy aircraft. This success was
widely acclaimed in the camp, for Spekie was very
popular, and we felt that his victory was in a way ours.
After this he went from strength to strength, scoring
quickly and well, and soon he was awarded the D.F.C.

Spekie was killed one afternoon in July. I was away,
and it was from the newspaper (the same which on
the day before had reported his D.F.C.) that I learnt
of this tragedy. It was hard to believe that Spekie was
dead. Had he been missing we would have expected
him back, although the chances would have been slender, but this time—as he had put it—this was it. We
would not see him again. Our loss was of a great friend,
a giant in character, completely unswerving in his
sense of duty, and always unselfish and considerate.
'Ask Spekie to do it for you' was the advice one got

[1] Wing Commander D. A. Jackson, O.B.E., D.F.C., A.F.C.
[2] Air Commodore C. H. Appleton, C.B.E., D.S.O., D.F.C.,
killed in action, August 12th, 1944.

when trying to find someone to take one's place on the operations programme, and unfailingly he would do it. He would volunteer to stand in for anyone at any time, to do an extra night's duty or to leave a comfortable bed and fly the very late patrol when the prospects of meeting the enemy were well known to be small. It was always he who first welcomed the new-comer and took trouble over lonely and apparently uninteresting people in the mess. 'One of Spekie's funny old friends' was a byword for someone who shared our mess but not our flying and whom we therefore considered beyond the pale, someone who was perhaps bored and unhappy until Spekie discovered him and introduced him into the snob circle of the operational crews. It was to him that the airmen would turn when they were in trouble, because they knew that they would get sympathy and, if it were humanly possible, help.

I was thankful that I was away. I imagined the glumness following earnest discussions about how it had happened. I would miss the box party (the R.A.F. name for a funeral) and the probable booze-up afterwards, when the dead man's friends tried to forget their loss and find oblivion and relaxation somehow, anyhow, as he would have wanted them to do. I knew that when I returned all that would be over and people would seem to have forgotten him; they would not refer to him. Then, months later, he would come back into the conversation, in a way immortal. And at Squadron gatherings for very long afterwards the first person whom the men would recall would be 'Mr. Speke'.

I saw him come into the crewroom with Derek that

night of his first success and, knowing him well, I realised that he was completely happy, as I had been, for he had achieved his ambition at last. He had no family to support, no dependants to be anxious about, and he had disliked an office life before, as he dreaded the prospect of it after, the war. He did not cling to this life and he was ready to die. His career was, in an important way, complete.

Chapter 9

COLTISHALL—TOUR EXPIRED

THE C.O. has a special place in one's esteem, for besides running the Squadron he is a member of one of the regular crews, sharing with them the successes and failures, the trials and tribulations of their pursuit—and surely it is this fellow feeling in adversity as well as in success, and the trust and dependence engendered by it, that are the foundation of all leadership. In August 1941 we lost a popular and respected C.O. and gained a worthy successor, for Charlie Appleton left the Squadron for a staff job and John Cunningham took over.

Such a change is always stirring, but here it was doubly so for me, since I was appointed to take over John's flight. I had already enjoyed in it, and in some way regretted leaving, the status of minimum responsibility, where such anxieties as there had been were always over matters under my immediate control. But now I would have to make decisions as John had done. I would have to decide when and in what weather the individual crews were fit to operate. John had a remarkable way with him; he seemed to nurse the crews, leading and yet quietly restraining them, until they began to assimilate and show some of his confidence, and were fit for operations in most weather. It would not be easy for his successor.

The flight moved at once to Coltishall in Norfolk,

to stand in while another squadron was equipped with Beaufighters. At that time there were frequent small raids on east coast towns, and sometimes enemy aircraft intruded, coming back with our bombers. We had been scoring well—the bag was now more than fifty—and having examined intact specimens of Junkers and Heinkels, we knew that it was hard for the Germans to maintain a good look-out. They would probably continue to be caught unawares. We were pleased with ourselves, and we thought that night fighting was all that mattered and that no squadron and no flight anywhere could rival ours. We had high hopes.

But once in Norfolk we could not help seeing that there was a great deal more developing in the air war than we were used to contemplate. Out over the North Sea we frequently intercepted, during those weeks, a Whitley or a Wellington going out or coming home, sailing along majestically, unconscious of our presence and completely alone, a dark shape against the sky, blotting out the stars, seen by us but not seeing us, carrying five men, heroes, I thought, every one of them. I hoped for them that the enemy had not begun to see in the dark, as we had.

Nevertheless, the excitement stayed (perhaps interception in the dark will never be commonplace) and I relapsed again into thinking only of my own efforts, and enjoying the limelight so liberally accorded to night-fighters—until I came across another 'friendly' bomber.

On the whole, we were disappointed with the results of our six weeks at Coltishall. Although more

than twenty aircraft were intercepted, all but five
turned out, on close inspection, to be 'friendly'. With
many 'friendly' aircraft coming and going, identities
often became mixed, and then there was nothing for
the fighter to do but go and have a look; and while he
was having a look at what turned out to be a Whitley
or Wellington, the enemy would get away unmolested.
Only three aircraft were destroyed, and these were all
caught by John and Jimmy, who again showed that
they had got something that we others had not got.
Two were destroyed in one night, and the second shot
back, hitting and putting an engine out of action.
Beaufighters were not easy to fly on one engine, but
judging by his composure after landing John had
taken the sixty-odd miles' limp home in his stride.

Stevens,[1] who had had the top score before these
successes, landed at Coltishall early one morning. His
had been a remarkable achievement, for he had destroyed thirteen enemy aircraft with no more assistance than his own intelligence and eyesight could give.
Operating freelance in a long-range Hurricane, he
flew as one possessed; he had a simple mission and
there were no conflicting interests. It was said that his
children had been killed in the blitz and that his wife
had lost her reason. He scorned Beaufighters and
radar, but we had interesting talks with him. He
recounted how one bomber which he had intercepted
had disintegrated with such an explosion after the first
few rounds that his machine was thrown on its back,
and he had to hurry down and land, suspecting serious

[1] Flight Lieutenant R. P. Stevens, D.S.O., D.F.C., killed in
action, December 15th, 1941.

damage. With some pride he pointed to the leading edge of the wing of his Hurricane; it was varnished but rough, as if sand had been sprinkled on it while it was still sticky, and he explained that what now looked like sand had been found there after that combat, and had been preserved on his instructions as a trophy both gruesome and illuminating. Stevens was killed not long afterwards. It was believed that he was 'shooting up' a searchlight post in France.

I intercepted but lost two enemy aircraft. I seemed incapable of doing the right thing at the right time. Perhaps these interceptions might have led to combats some months before, but now they ended in fiasco. I saw the first enemy twice; the first time I was well placed below and about 300 yards away, but was closing in too fast. I throttled back and lowered the undercarriage. The aircraft ahead of me had first been described as a 'bogey', that is, unidentified and to be investigated with caution, and, believing that I could hold it in sight, I asked quickly for more news; but it was still a 'bogey'. During the few seconds taken by that conversation I was cut off from my observer and, had he been able to speak to me, he could have warned me of what was to become apparent immediately afterwards. He could have warned me that I had slowed down too much, that the aircraft ahead was drawing away and that the shapeless blob, seen only because it obliterated the stars, would soon disappear. I lost sight of that aircraft, and so had impressed on me once more how the electric could be superior to the human eye. I closed in and saw it again, this time from above and to one side. Again I was overshooting;

to avoid going ahead and losing the contact, I pulled away farther to the side, and climbed in order to lose distance and speed. Again I lost sight of it, but still it was a 'bogey' and still we had a contact. Again I closed in, but this time I could not get a sight of it and, suspecting that I had overshot, I broke away and fell back to try and come in more steadily. Several times this happened and once I believed I was seeing exhaust flames dead ahead, but the radar indicated that my target was moving over to port. I believed that I had learnt my lesson, and I doubted my eyes and trusted the radar. Stars can look like exhausts just as exhausts can look like stars (and near the horizon stars can even look like tail-lights—we had named one star after a member of the Squadron who once chased it with high hopes), and this time I was not going to be taken in. But my trust in the radar had that time been misplaced, for there were no results, and after nearly thirty minutes the contact was finally lost and I went home dejected, mortified, full of self-recrimination and convinced that it was an enemy who had been so close to me.

The next day the radar in that aircraft was tested and was found to be fickle. We found that a target seemed to be swinging slowly from port to starboard or vice versa when it was in fact remaining dead ahead. The exhaust flames had in all probability really been there, and the only right course would have been to have doubted the radar at that particular moment and to have believed what I thought I saw; but my eyes were tired after so much intensive peering, and I had doubted them and that aircraft went on to bomb Hull.

There was another mistake a few nights later when I came out from a cloud in full moonlight and, seeing an aircraft which was probably hostile crossing my course, went back into the cloud again in the hope of re-emerging behind him undetected. The aircraft passed close above me as I was trying to readjust myself to flying on instruments, and it quickly passed out of our small effective radar range. These were losses of opportunity which might have been excusable in a new crew, but I had not this excuse. It seemed that I was losing the power to co-ordinate thought and action in the unique way that would earn success, and I began to wonder whether what they called operational tiredness was not beginning to show itself.

My flying had begun now and again to alarm me. I noticed sometimes an inattention to detail and a wandering of attention, which were, I knew, abnormal. One dark night I found myself at 200 feet when I believed I was safe at a thousand, and although I had been distracted by difficulty in lowering the undercarriage, such carelessness was new. Thus, it struck me at the time, did some experienced pilots kill themselves and their crews. "Odd," they would have said the next day (or even on the same night), "he had lots of experience. I can't imagine what happened." I believed I would be all right when I had had some leave.

Some, taking night flying in their stride, never showed signs of fatigue, while others did not last long. Most of us though, the average majority, using up our nervous energy at our own characteristic rates, needed (and got) regular breaks for recovery. I used to hope that nervous energy need never run out, like the sands in an hour-glass, if properly watched. I wanted no change, and asked nothing more than to fly until the end of the war.

Our work was tiring, and though not fraught with danger it was often exacting, for we now flew in most weathers. At Coltishall our routine was four nights on duty out of seven. There was not much let-up; the days were full and alike. I would get up late, breakfast at eleven, visit the office at twelve to make out the programme for the night's flying and to deal with minor administrative matters, lunch, go to the hangars again, fly my own machine for that night and test all its equipment, have tea and, with luck, an hour or two of peace and quiet before an early dinner, unless there was a further test flight to be made. By now the tempo would be increasing fast. I would return to the hangars, put on my flying-clothes, have a word with the controller, go out with my observer to the aircraft, get in, and be strapped in and then shut in. And now, at about eight-fifteen at this season, was the zenith; it was dusk. The worst was over and I was committed to fly. The horrid little hope that the weather might be too bad had been abandoned and the rest was inevitable.

The engines started and the machine trundled out to the flare-path. There was a moment's hesitation for final checks, and it moved off, gathering speed with a widespread commotion like thunder. In an exciting surge of speed, it charged down the runway. The bumping lessened and ceased, and we were airborne. Climbing hard and guided only by a voice, we left the earth far behind to regain it only after a two to three hours' vigil. Ahead there might be anything from the utter boredom of an uneventful patrol to the priceless drama of a combat; and the setting might be clear, dark and splendid, or limpid, gentle and nearly as light as day; or, as it sometimes was, so solid, opaque and unpleasant that after a while, with the instrument dials seeming to dance and electricity flashing across the windscreen, a disembodied yet frightened feeling made a return to Mother Earth seem in a way remote.

After our spell it would come at last, 'Return to base and pancake', and we would go down, down, down, perhaps into cloud. 'You may come straight in'; and then with great care we would carry out the usual landing drill, going out from base on zero nine zero to ten miles and turning slowly to two seven zero, the alignment of the runway. 'Ten miles dead ahead.' (Reduce to a thousand feet and look out.) There, two miles ahead, was the airfield brilliantly lit up, the runway, the funnel lights, the outer circuit lights, the glide-path indicators; every possible aid. (Wheels down, flaps down—start holding off—throttle back.) Crump! Once again we were on terra firma. It was much easier than it used to be. Now there were 2,000 yards of runway, lavish lighting and a regulated way of getting down, a reliable and familiar blind-approach system.

I might be down by midnight, and I would have supper while the machine was being refuelled. Satisfied that I had done my duty for the night, I would hope for relaxation in the state of 'readiness', so that I could go to bed. By two or three I might get back to the mess to bed. I would sleep late next morning, get up late and my day had begun again. Sometimes I forgot the day of the week; one day was very like another. I began to feel an inertia. Perhaps the hour-glass analogy was wrong.

Our time at Coltishall came to an end and I had some leave. Back at Middle Wallop, the winter came and began to drag through. There was little enemy activity, and still we kept up our nightly sentry-go. One day in January John said to me in his quiet way, "Rory, I have been told to find another flight commander. You are going to Persia." And so I left the Squadron.

Chapter 10

STAFF WORK

PLANS were changed, as they had been before, and I did not go to Persia. I stayed at Middle Wallop, and I became a fighter controller, an experience which was instructive and chastening for one who, as a sort of prima donna, had helped to make the controllers' task a thankless one. A few weeks later I was posted, and I found myself a staff officer in a Group Headquarters, with the function of organising the training of new night-fighter crews.

The headquarters was in Gloucestershire in a sham Elizabethan house. To redress its inadequacy as a headquarters, huts had been built, and they sprawled offensively over part of the grounds. In spite of all the ugliness, the impression made on me in March was that the place would be lovely in summer, and so my relegation to a desk lost some of its sting. The house stood on the south side of a small valley which fell away westwards from the higher ground. There was a spring up there, and a stream from it flowed down through the well-kept gardens, swelling out to a lily-pond in which there were trout. A tennis-court and a kitchen garden completed the picture of this headquarters of a fighter-training Group.

Summer came and early on I had my table and chair moved to a back room—such changes were of importance to a staff officer—for this strange house faced north and the plentiful sunshine of 1942 was reaching me only in the very late afternoon. Thereafter my office work was done with the sun often on my back, and in the gay company of three others who, like myself, were for the time being 'on the shelf'. There I tried to learn about minute writing, 'usual channels', their uses and abuses, and the paper work that goes with staff duties.

I visited fighter-training stations, and I learnt that there was another aspect of staff work. Stations had been left much to themselves to train night-fighter crews as they thought fit, and in consequence the headquarters' assumption of authority to direct policy and methods was unpopular. Enthusiasts—many of them in those days inexperienced in operations—had worked out their own plans, and they did not like changing them. But some had to be changed. There was a limit to the flying hours which could be devoted to the training of each crew, and into this time had to be packed as many as possible of the lessons learnt, in this new realm, since the war began.

This work was as interesting as it was at times frustrating. One station commander would listen politely and act, another would only listen, and one, I recall, would hardly deign even to listen.

Staff work in general remained a mystery to me, and I was not to understand its major implications until several years later when I was again floundering as a staff officer—but at that time in deeper water. Then, tied to an office and deprived of many contacts, I saw the value of its paper relations; the point of 'usual channels', minutes and 'putting it on record' became very clear.

My parish was big, and to visit it I had to fly the length of the country. These visits to training stations could be welcome and cheering outings and, when sitting for too long in an office had bred in me a feeling of ineffectiveness and despondency, I liked to get out and find encouragement and reassurance in their enthusiastic activity. To be divorced from active flying and to sit instead in an office, trying to plan, was depressing at times. There were the temptations that may produce the 'drunks' of the next war. To live normal hours, to have every night off and no longer to experience the fear and subsequent elation—the triumph of getting back on to the ground in one piece—will dissatisfy a tour-expired pilot and he will long for the old excitement; but as a staff officer he can often fly, for his work may take him all over the country, and that sort of flying can also be absorbing. On my outings, I learnt the geography of the country well. Weather reports were often misleading, and the surest way of getting about was to go and see for oneself; a start was always worthwhile provided it was possible to get back to the starting-point, and familiarity with the ground was essential for this. Picking my way, even in fair weather, never far from a railway-line to which I could turn in bad visibility, I would break the flight up into easily memorised sections, and on all of these I knew or could soon learn my exact position. Getting about thus in bad weather was sometimes exciting, but it was satisfying to get there and confound the gloomiest forecaster. Everyday flying offered experiences as varied as the colours of the spectrum, and some will never fade.

One day I left the Highlands for East Fortune, near Edinburgh, in a rainstorm. It was midsummer, but all day rainstorms had been interspersed with spells when the sun struggled and prevailed through ragged clouds. This weather looked good enough, and I had decided to go and see for myself. I was flying in a Tiger Moth, the most modest of contemporary machines; thus I was in the open air. It was raining hard when I took off, but it was a shower and at a few hundred feet I was out of it. There were more patches of rain on the hills ahead. Gingerly I looked for and found the railway, the 'iron beam', whose sinuous course I might have to follow all the way. In a few minutes I saw that the rain on the hills, which had appeared menacing from the ground, did not extend far. On either side the air was clear, so clear that there seemed to be no limit to the range of visibility. To the left I could see blue sky and to the right was a shaft of sunlight slanting through the clouds, while ahead were further rainstorms and sunlit patches. The colours of the mountains stood out better in that light and shade than they would have done in full sunlight. The scale of this inconceivably beautiful scene was right. The mountains, so dominant to the earthbound, were beaten by this little flying machine. I now skimmed over them, gliding sometimes between them, following a river, crossing a well-known road and meeting the railway again.

After four months rumour reached me that I was being moved. It was soon confirmed, and I was posted to Ford to a small night-fighter trials unit. I was to be promoted. John was extracted from the Squadron to take over from me. Together we visited the stations, and on the evening of our return I went down to Ford to see my predecessor there.

To be caught in the dark, out of flying practice, in a small machine which had no radio, was my reward for leaving my departure until too late. Dusk was not far off when I left, but I hoped to be well on the way before it became quite dark; and, anyhow, the weather was fine and Ford was easy to find. That is what I thought before I took off, but as soon as I was airborne I began to doubt the wisdom of this cross-country flying without wireless. To go on in the gloom seemed, in those first moments, rash. I had better go back and land while there was some light; but I was unable to. I went on, but sought reassurance by groping for the parachute and harness. I asked myself what I was scared about. I knew where I was; I should be at Ford in about thirty minutes. But there is a break between day and night flying that brings qualms and foreboding, and it was now beginning to look very dark; I was not seeing the ground ahead. Soon I could see nothing more of the ground and I had to give up peering. What might happen? Would it be possible to miss Ford? Then there would be a panicky search with the risk of never following any plan for sufficient time, like a chicken in front of a motor-car. It might be like an adventure of 1930 when, in an Avro 504 and airborne alone for the third time, I lost myself within a mile or two of Hendon. Then, in daylight, I had made two hair-raising forced landings before I found an aerodrome; but now it was dark.

These thoughts jostled through my mind and gave way to saner ones. On this clear night I could not miss a coastline, and Ford and Tangmere lights would surely be visible from several miles. Thus I began to enjoy myself and, as the stars came out, I realised that I was night flying. Before long I saw lights that winked and others that soon became circuit lights; the red beacon told me that ahead was Ford, and I saw the curves of the River Arun, which were to become so familiar in the coming months. I wondered why we did not fly more at night in these little aeroplanes, which had no radio to intrude on our almost perfect privacy. I was signalled in and I landed with some reluctance. As I drove to the mess I wondered whether I had been wise or foolhardy not to turn back while there was sufficient light, and I concluded that had I not been able to land at Ford I would have been foolhardy; but in the outcome I had been wise because I was now, at a stroke, in practice and confident. I had been reminded that there was nothing to fear from the dark, and the next night I flew back from Hendon to Gloucestershire, leaving at dusk and arriving in the dark. Then I had not even momentary qualms, and again I enjoyed a unique sort of privacy.

Chapter 11

DEVELOPMENT

WE had started the war with no effective night defence, and the enemy, when beaten back in daylight, had been able to mount heavy and damaging attacks at night with negligible losses. Only once during the 'blitz' had his losses been heavy, and then, in an attack on London, he learnt the lesson that we were to learn later (and often at heavy cost) that an aircraft, illuminated from above by the moon, and from below by a burning city and silhouetted against cloud, is easily picked up at long range by the naked eye. On that night our day fighters, flying in conditions most favourable to them, had destroyed more than thirty bombers. Yet this was an isolated case, and generally enemy losses cannot have been of much significance. The improvement of our defence at night had had top priority, and even when there was little sting left in the enemy bombing effort, the effect of that programme continued.

The formidable scale of the problem can be seen when day and night interception methods are compared, since the aim was, in essence, to turn night into day. In daylight a number of fighters, from a section of two to a wing of thirty-six, was under one control. The pilots could see a medium-sized aircraft from ten miles or so if the sky was clear, and the hawk-eyed might see it at twelve or fifteen miles. They could scan the horizon, look all around and size up the dispositions of the aircraft (though not, of course, at that range their identities). From about ten miles away the battle was all theirs, and the controller, his job done, could wish them luck.

At night, instead of many fighters, one only was controlled. Sightings were denied to the pilots until they were very close, and the early radar (though in some ways superior) was at first a poor substitute for eyesight, for its range was seldom greater than five miles (it depended in the early types on height) and its perception of a change in course, immediate with the naked eye, was late. Thus the attention of the ground control had to be close, individual and continuous, and the system had a low capacity (a weakness from which searchlight control did not suffer to the same extent). There could be no support by other fighters such as was possible in daylight, and success or failure hung on the sometimes uncertain performances of one aircraft, its equipment and crew. Concentration in a raid, embarrassing enough to the defence in daylight, was much more so at night when the defences could be more easily saturated. This was later exploited to the full in our bomber offensive.

By June 1942 when I was posted to Ford, there had been changes. The enemy had changed his tactics. Spasmodic raiding had been kept up, and in such senseless operations as the so-called Baedeker raid on Bath, the bombers had been elusive, flying in fast, changing height frequently, keeping a good look-out and maintaining regular evasive action. Such tactics had been effective against our Beaufighters, whose radar did not give early perception of these moves and so made the chances of sighting and attack remote; but the effect on the enemy's navigation was often disastrous, and many of them, hopelessly lost, never reached their targets. A few (in the slang of 1945 they would have been called 'press-on types') were shot down. They were probably among the more resolute, who flew more or less straight and level, determined to reach their targets.

There had been a remarkable development in fighter radar. By using shorter waves and narrow beams, it was becoming more perceptive and its range was increasing. The early drawback of the dependence of its range on height was being overcome. Control of the operation could be transferred earlier to the fighter, and defence capacity was thus increased. The Mosquito was coming into service and showed marked advances on the Beaufighter. Although its initial rate of climb was not so good, its manœuvrability, ceiling, and top speed were considerably better; it had no vices.

The ground-control system had also been improved. A multiplication of the radar stations of the sort which had proved their worth in the hands of the scientists who had designed them, now provided a thin defensive screen of individually controlled fighters all round our coast. Inland, radar-guided searchlights were deployed, and other fighters were available to work with them, providing another line of defence. Over the target radar-guided guns had a free hand.

In this sketch of our problems mention has to be

made of the greatest—identification. The parallel of daylight interception shows the fighter pilot weighing up an air situation from afar. He sees what he believes is an enemy bomber ten miles away; his eyes cannot gauge the range with accuracy, and he cannot be sure from that range that the aircraft he sees is a hostile bomber. Coming closer, he begins to be able to estimate the range and he tries to make a recognition. The controller would have told him that the aircraft was hostile or unknown. Before attacking, he has to identify the aircraft for himself, and he would do it by recognising its shape, features and markings. He would have time to form a conclusion.

But at night there were embarrassing complications. The ground control did not have the help which it could obtain in daylight from the Observer Corps, who were able to identify most of the aircraft they were able to see. At night the air 'picture', seen by ground radar and reported by the Observer Corps, was largely quantitative, weakly qualitative, and never so clear as it was by day. While our aircraft could use radar to identify themselves to our ground stations (by means of an automatically transmitted signal which would be associated with the radar echo seen by the ground station), this system was notoriously unreliable, and fighters were not infrequently sent to intercept aircraft which turned out to be 'friendly'.

On a dark night the fighter pilot would not see another aircraft of medium size until within three to four hundred yards. Closer he would see it as an uncertain and shapeless blot, an area of obliterated starlight, but he could not recognise it and he had to go much closer, to 100 yards probably, before it took on a recognisable shape. He was unable to see its markings, and so all depended on his quick recognition of a shape which was two dimensional and had no depth, a true silhouette. If this shape was found eventually to be that of a 'friendly', the time spent in interception and recognition had been wasted, and the enemy would have got through, in all probability unmolested. Reliable aids to longer-range identification between aircraft were badly needed.

One experimental system employed intermittent infra-red light transmissions from a lamp on the aircraft's tail. These were invisible to the naked eye. They could be seen by the fighter by means of a special receiver, and they could be coded to show the morse letters of the day or period. This was to provide identification of friendly aircraft beyond the range at which a silhouette could be recognised, without the disadvantages inherent in the use of visible light signals, visible to friend and foe alike. Though cumbersome, this system was effective, and it was to be invaluable later when our fighters were operating against German fighters and had to avoid chasing one another. Another system, which made use of dim-coloured lights let into the rear of the wings near the tips, and visible only from astern and (theoretically) only at close range, was already in use in 1942, but it was understandably unpopular.

The absence of these lights, visible or invisible, or, later on, of certain radar signals transmitted between aircraft (on the same principle as the air-to-ground signals already mentioned), did not suffice to identify the aircraft pursued as hostile beyond all doubt. It added only to the suspicions as to its character. Visual recognition would complete the case, and was demanded, though it was not always possible, and the evidence had sometimes to be weighed up and a decision made without this final and satisfying confirmation. Accidents occurred in daylight when false identifications were made, but many more—it will never be known how many—were made at night, and night identification was to remain one of the biggest problems of the night air war.

Our night-fighter formula was now established. The twin-engined two-seater carrying radar, petrol for five hours and an armament of four 20-millimetre cannon conclusively proved itself the best. The single-seater, which had scored such a success on that one night over London, and which, in the hands of unique pilots like Stevens, had done so well even on dark nights, was disappearing. A single-seater had been fitted with radar, but the two-seater, in which two brains dealt with the problem, was deemed better. Another defence method, discarded after a prolonged and extensive trial which had culminated in the death of an air-raid warden in a provincial city, was to drop in front of raiders as an aerial minefield a network of explosives hanging from parachutes. And finally there was the airborne searchlight, carried by a radar-equipped machine which was accompanied by satellite fighters. This was a costly experiment, which seemed ill-timed to those who believed in the Beaufighter or Mosquito, for by the time that the Turbinlite—as it was called— appeared, Beaufighters were showing a form which argued strongly that that formula was the best, at least for some time to come.

An early disappearance from the front line was that of the Defiant. As a night-fighter it had been in some ways ideal, and it had been popular in this rôle with its crews. With a crew of two it carried four machine-guns in a turret which could be brought to bear on an aircraft at the maximum range at which the latter was visible, and at a range at which the attacker against the darker background remained invisible. It carried no radar and its successes were not many. With one engine it was too slow, and by the time that a faster radar-carrying Defiant was being considered, the Mosquito was on the way and the project was dropped.

It was perhaps fortunate that limitations in design and production did not allow multiplication of our aircraft types in this field. There was a case in favour of the single-seater, the two-seater and even the three-seater night-fighter. Some demanded manoeuvrability and accepted short duration; while others required greater duration, the ability to carry a heavier long-range radar set and a crew to share the tasks. All were in favour of armament such as that of the Defiant which, besides being able to fire upwards and so ex-ploit the maximum ranges of visibility, was also mov-able; and all agreed that the fixed guns firing along the fighter's axis, though desirable because of their heavy calibre, made it much harder to score hits, since at the moment of aiming the target was silhouetted against the horizon, which was usually the darkest part of the sky. Everyone agreed, too, that radar was essential.

But the all-purpose defensive and, later, offensive night-fighter was to be the Mosquito, an aircraft whose superlative design provided all the manœuvrability any pilot could want at night, a flight duration of more than six hours, a second seat (beside the pilot) for a radar operator (later to become also a navigator), and the ability to carry the most powerful radar and four 20-millimetre cannon, fixed and firing along the machine's axis. Since many regretted the lack of upward-firing guns, one experimental Mosquito was built with a turret, but fortunately it was unsatisfactory and no further effort was diverted to spoiling the Mosquitoes.

The history of fighter development shows how the first fighters had free guns in the form of shot-guns or pistols wielded by the observer. The time soon came, however, when the fixed gun, firing through the propeller, was developed, and as time went on and the fighter versus fighter competition started, the front fixed gun prevailed, since it allowed guns of increasing calibre to be mounted in single-seaters without detracting from their performance, as did a turret with movable guns protruding into and firing across the slip-stream. The fixed-gun fighter remained supreme.

At night the only thought had been for the interception and destruction of bombers, and for this the Beaufighter and Mosquito had more than adequate speed. The addition of a turret to either would certainly have reduced their speed, but could perhaps have been justified by better and surer shooting. But there then appeared the enemy night-fighter-bomber,

' The Mosquito was coming into service . . .'
The Mosquito Mark II, equipped with A.I. Mark IV

Imperial War Museum

' . . . a second seat (beside the pilot)
The cockpit of a Mosquito equipped with A.I. Mark VIII

'. . . a valuable landmark in bad weather as one flew along the coast . . .'
The mouth of the river Arun at Littlehampton

the Focke Wulf 190 and the Messerschmitt 410, which came in high and fast from France, dropped their bombs and scuttled off. The Mosquito was suddenly opposed by fighters, and the fact that it acquitted itself well is attributable not only to its design but also to the fact that the protagonists of the free gun had not prevailed and the Mosquito's speed had remained unimpaired. When towards the end of the war Mosquitoes flew in large numbers over Germany with the object of harassing the enemy night-fighters, it was their speed and manœuvrability which allowed the Mosquitoes, hundreds of miles from their bases, to make full use of their superior radar, and to give such a good account of themselves as to earn, among enemy night-fighter crews, an almost legendary reputation.

Chapter 12

FORD

IN 1940 a small unit had been formed for the pur-
pose of testing new interception equipment and
tactics in operations; it started its work at Manston
and later found a home at Ford. In June 1942 I was
given command of it.

As an aerodrome Ford left little to be desired. The
approaches were good from east and west, and com-
pensating for the Downs to the north were the sea to
the south and the Arun River which flowed close by, a
valuable landmark in bad weather as one flew along
the coast. Its situation was perfect, with Arundel,
dominated by a church and a castle, a mile or two
away. Its weather seemed better than in most parts;
there was no industrial haze and it was often clear
when other parts were clouded over. When south-
bound, we would often find that cloud broke and disappeared once the Downs were passed. These, the
physical assets, were not Ford's only advantages for,
besides being comfortable to live on and unexcelled to
fly from, it was also a supremely happy station. Its
spirit, which was enjoyed alike by visitors and by those
of the station, reflected well the personality of Gerald
Maxwell[1], its commander.

As a fighter pilot in the Kaiser's war, Gerald had
destroyed more than thirty enemy aircraft. He had

[1] Wing Commander G. C. Maxwell, M.C., D.F.C., A.F.C.

left the service but had never lost his love for it, and with Hitler's war imminent he joined the Auxiliaries. By way of a balloon squadron and the Air Ministry, he came eventually to Fighter Command Headquarters, whence he came to Ford as station commander. People interested him, and he made them all feel that they mattered to him, as indeed they did. He took an enthusiastic interest in all the activities of the station; it was a point of honour with him to fly all types of aircraft and, besides the station commander's Moth, which was often to be seen in the vicinity of Ford executing perfect aerobatics (Gerald had toured America after the first war on an official goodwill flying mission), he flew solo practically every type that landed at Ford.

I found myself in command of a unit of about twenty officers and two hundred men. It had great *esprit de corps*, and my predecessors had set high standards; it was hand-picked, to some extent privileged, and influential. At the time of my arrival it had Beaufighters, Mosquitoes, a Spitfire, a Hurricane, a Magister and a Hornet Moth, besides some odd aircraft on loan; it had its own motor transport, which included a shooting-brake primarily for the use of its commanding officer. It had one end of the airfield to itself, and there were ample offices, hangars and crew rooms.

It was the established practice that after a certain amount of operational flying, crews would be moved to training or staff duties; and they usually hated both. By a special dispensation and because our flying would not all be in operations, our crews could be drawn from those described as 'tour expired', their time at

Ford counting as a rest period. Thus the unit was much sought after and it was possible to enlist in its complement of twelve aircrew men who, besides being well experienced in operations, had other qualifications appropriate to its work.

Our reports carried great weight, for the testing of new equipment in squadrons had been abandoned when it had caused delays and produced conflicting reports, and ours had become the only operational trials. Policy decisions might be made on our verdict, and each crew and each member of the crew had to be able to report objectively on aircraft, equipment and tactics, never forgetting the capacities of average pilots and observers.

There was much scope for controversy. Team-work between a pilot and an observer was the key to success in this groping in the dark, and its form depended on the balance between them. There were pilots who left themselves entirely in the hands of their observers, following unquestioningly every instruction given, and there were others who insisted on being told only the position of the other aircraft relative to themselves. Most preferred a compromise, a running commentary on the situation as seen by the radar, and instructions on what to do. There were some pilots who, anxious for a greater degree of control, greatly welcomed a type of radar with an indicator in the cockpit which gave the pilot information about the intercepted aircraft's position. There were others who equally greatly abhorred this principle, avowing that the pilot should all the time be looking outside and not into the cockpit. We had to tread warily.

The nature of much of our work was to change as the emphasis in the air war changed from defence to attack. By then much of the purely defensive equipment had reached a stage from which it would not need much development for some time to come. We had the aircraft, the radar, the guns and the gunsights; there was not much more of importance that had to be done immediately. And so we were able to devote much effort to co-operation with our counterpart bomber unit in testing equipment for bomber defence and developing effective evasive tactics. Night-time would find bombers being chased all over the sky in the vicinity of Ford trying out radar tail-warning and other devices. Trailing along behind the bombers we observed the effect, or lack of effect, on us of a flash let off by the rear gunner as soon as he had seen us, and we followed them at all heights, falling back and closing in to determine the visibility ranges of the exhausts, a trial which produced alarming results and added even more to one's fears for our bomber crews. The work on evasive tactics was to bear fruit some time later, when the two units developed the corkscrew manœuvre for bombers. This, it was confirmed to me by the top-scoring German night-fighter pilot, was wholly effective; he had followed a corkscrewing Lancaster once for forty-five minutes without once having a chance of shooting. In this way fighter knowledge was capitalised and applied to the bomber offensive, a slogging match so different from the war we knew.

In the direction of our activities we were fortunate, being responsible to Fighter Command and getting our instructions from Hicko,[1] an erstwhile member of the unit, an Auxiliary and now a staff officer. Hicko dealt out the jobs and was our general mentor. He got us the best crews and aircraft, and he kept the wolves at bay. Covetous eyes fell on our Hornet Moth, the nicest and most sociable of all small aeroplanes, to which we were much attached, but in the end we kept it; and now and again an attempt would be made to replace the shooting-brake (a Chevrolet) by the smallest of Hillmans; it would become immobilised, and Hicko would be appealed to with all despatch. We kept it till the end. And it was Hicko who had been instrumental in rescuing me from the bogus Elizabethan headquarters where I had been masquerading as a staff officer.

Ford was two hours by car, or a little over an hour by electric train, from London. Our mess was not only comfortable and warm but, being in a country house which had formerly been used as a school, its interior and exterior were pleasantly unorthodox. A small bar had been installed, and in that room there was an old and beer-stained piano; and there was always talent in the sort of songs which are most appropriate to mess bars. On rare occasions Gerald played the piano for us.

In April 1943 I went to America for five weeks, an absorbing and welcome distraction, for at Ford the lack of action had begun to overshadow the interest of the work. We were flying regularly on defensive patrols, but even an attempted interception of an enemy had become an event. I had hurried back, but I found the situation, for us, unchanged—and there was much

[1] Group Captain R. H. Hiscox, C.B.E.

going on to make one discontented with inactivity.

Now we had the equipment and the technique, but we could not use it. In my own mind I felt the beginnings of a hopelessness reminiscent of the early spring of 1941, when we had the equipment and the opponents but lacked the technique. But now, as then, I was to be abnormally fortunate.

Plans were discussed for offensive operations, but they all foundered on the same rocks. Our function was to fly experimentally, and we were all abreast of the latest developments in our particular sphere. Any one of us might, with Nazi treatment, give away vital information—one had to admit that—and so we were not allowed to fly over enemy-occupied territory. This was logical and it could not be disputed, but there was a risk that our inactivity in the midst of great activity would be damaging to morale.

One July evening I flew to a Suffolk airfield to attend a station party. I asked to be excused early, since I was on the operational programme, a plan which would allow me to leave a function that I did not expect to enjoy. I left at nine forty-five, and half an hour later I was sitting in our crew-room at 'readiness'. Gerald came in on his evening rounds and we gossiped a bit. I became restless and telephoned once more to the operations-room to ask whether there was any sign of enemy activity. The controller replied that there were no indications of it, and he thought that there was no point even in flying a precautionary patrol. It would be better to stay at 'readiness' on the ground since the weather was not all it might be—a cautious and reasonable proposition.

To feel useless was bad enough, but to have this feeling confirmed that way made it worse. What had been suggested would have meant not even earning my daily bread. And so I suggested a patrol to keep myself in practice and to exercise the control stations, by then well overlapping each other in their fields of vision, a continuous screen round the coast. We would fly through them, talking to and being plotted by one after another, being handed from one to another as we passed from one field of vision to the next. The weather was good enough—I had no qualms on that score—and I wanted to keep up my morale, to be released after flying instead of spending the rest of the night at 'readiness' in the crew-room, and to give some practice to the control stations in a technique which needed practice.

We went off in a Mosquito at about 1 a.m. The weather was fair; there was a haze up to 4,000 feet, but above it was a clear but very dark, moonless night. Side by side, as if we were sitting in a carriage, Bamford,[1] my observer, and I flew up the coast, bowing, as it were, to acquaintances as we passed, calling up the control stations, being told by the first to pass on and then changing frequency and calling the next one. The first hand-over was done clumsily and it seemed to me that there was a lack of keenness—it was, after all, after 1 a.m.—and as petulant pilots were apt to do, I slated them roundly, exhorting them to wake up and imagine that there was an enemy about. Ten minutes later, when I must have been somewhere near

[1] Flying Officer N. L. Bamford, D.F.C., killed on active service, January 1st, 1945.

Hastings under the control of a voice which I did not know, I was told to turn about and fly west; there was what was then described as a 'customer', which meant that something suspicious had been seen. It might be a flock of geese or a thunder cloud or, more probably, an aeroplane; and so—described soon as a 'bandit'—it was. While I followed the instructions automatically, hardly believing such startling news, it flashed through my mind how appropriate it would be if this were a hoax, a thunder cloud or a flock of geese that disappeared—but that was unthinkable.

I went through it all again, in reverse this time, and was handed over from one station to the next as I flew west. The 'bandit' was about forty miles away, and with plenty of time to think and wonder I became confident. I had had phenomenal luck before, and it might happen again.

The 'bandit' was flying north and very low. I was told to reduce height as much as I could. Fortunately my Mosquito had a radio altimeter, a device which gave absolute readings of height. Instructions were given to turn on to courses of 300, 340 and then 360 degrees. I could picture the plan of the interception. Then the 'bandit' turned east, and I was given, in quick succession, 60 and then 90 degrees. We were getting close and, so I was told, could expect a contact imminently.

I was well aware of the need to fly low. The radar in my aircraft was of a type that searched, scanning the horizon, the sky and the ground or sea. The echo from an aircraft below us would be mixed up with echoes from the sea or the land and hard to distinguish from them, but an echo from above would be 'seen' alone against the echo-less background of the sky. Thus to 'see' this aircraft clearly we had to get down below it early on. There was haze and it was pitch dark. Low flying had to be done on instruments, and to force the height down to 300 and 200 feet, an all too enjoyable altitude in daylight, went against all the normal instincts of self-preservation.

Suddenly a contact appeared at two miles and, vainly hoping that there was something to be seen, I looked ahead. The contact was lost and I had to ask the control for more help. They gave me another vector, 180°, and told me that I was still fairly close. I glanced at the altimeter and found that I had climbed to 800 feet—the automatic effect of a nervous hand on the control column. Concentrating now only on the instruments, I applied myself to getting low again, and in a few minutes my observer picked out another contact.

We were now flying fast towards France and towards the limit of the ground-control station's 'vision'. It would have to be now or never. My observer clung on, peering at his tube and persevering, seeing the echo more clearly as I got the better of my funk through great concentration and the radio altimeter, and then seeing it become less distinct, swamped by sea 'returns' as I looked ahead excitedly and we gained height. Like most observers, Bamford made no complaint, but suffered his pilot's weakness stoically and cheerfully.

Eventually—it seemed long since we had started this chase—we had a firm contact and were closing in comfortably. At a mile it was always worth having a look and I began to look ahead intently. The night, as I have said, was pitch black, and there were no stars visible except well above the horizon; and so it was that a point of light ahead aroused my curiosity. It was well above the horizon but isolated. No, it did not look like a star. I kept my eyes on it and increased speed. The radar contact was maintained, and it told us that we were overhauling our quarry fast. The point of light became two, and the correlation of their movements with the information from my observer confirmed that they came from an aircraft. At 200 yards the two points of light became four, and round them appeared a silhouette of a two-engined aircraft, made vague by the dazzle from the exhausts.

This was the hell of a problem. The sole chance of making a positive recognition was by seeing the plan silhouette, but that meant going down a hundred feet or so, and although we were now a bit higher I was not going down when I could not keep an eye on the altimeter. But all the circumstantial evidence pointed to this aircraft being hostile. Its engines had two rows of exhausts each, and that suggested a Junkers 88, as did its speed; it carried no recognition lights; it had appeared from the direction of France, flying very low, had come to within a few miles of our coast and was now heading back in the direction of France; it had been referred to by the control in all but the very first instance as a 'bandit'. Had I to risk all to complete the case? Should I perhaps follow it until it crossed the French coast—but that was forbidden for radar fighters. And would even that give more positive identification than I already had? Or should I weigh up the evidence now and act on it? And, anyhow, what was positive identification? The enemy sometimes flew captured aircraft, as we did (it was confirmed after their defeat that this had been commoner than we thought), and in the last resort could not a Wellington, for example, be followed until preparation to land at an enemy airfield showed it to be hostile despite its silhouette? This was hair-splitting; the sooner the job was done the better. I told my observer to look ahead and came up level. I opened fire from about 200 yards, aiming between the tell-tale exhausts. I saw some strikes and drew away to the left.

A light came on amidships and there was return fire; it went wide of the mark. Now I knew as certainly as I ever would know that this machine was a Junkers 88. I came in astern again and a second burst produced a small explosion in the fuselage. Suddenly it slowed down and I found myself overtaking alarmingly. I pulled the stick back and sailed up and over, climbing steeply. Almost simultaneously there was a blinding flash. Dazzled, I sat tight and eased the stick forward. When I could see again I flattened out unsteadily and began to wonder what had happened, for on the spur of the moment I was unable to connect the events in an intelligible sequence. As we collected our wits we realised what had happened, because there was a pool of fire on the sea. We circled over it once or twice, called up and reported the combat, accepted and reciprocated congratulations, and went back to land at 0235 hours, having at least for that night earned our keep.

Part Two

ATTACK

Chapter 13

THE BOMBERS

OUR bomber raids were now massive and concentrated. Forces of many hundred four-engined aircraft operated whenever the weather allowed, and the scale of attack was mounting. Sometimes they would go out over Ford and often they would land back there. It was not uncommon for twenty or thirty of them to come in, diverted from their own bases because of bad weather. Amongst them were always some lame ducks scrambling in somehow and ending up through a hedge with no brakes, or prone with an undercarriage that collapsed or would not come down, or by good fortune on their wheels and neatly parked near the perimeter track awaiting the repair squads. Sometimes there was a disaster and a machine, already home, crashed for reasons unknown and without survivors.

The Nazis were being hit hard and in the only way open to us. The brave policy of the four-engined weight-lifting bombers was very appropriate to the war at this stage. They went out at night unescorted, using the dark as their cover as the enemy had done, and their losses in these relatively early days, though mounting, were not excessive. Opposing defences were being built up, and the enemy had more leeway to make up than we had had (one wonders if it had ever seriously occurred to the Nazis that they might one day have to fight in the air at night).

We, the night-fighter boys, had been accustomed to being, as we thought, in the centre of the stage. We had, in fact, been there for a time after the Battle of Britain, when the miracle of airborne radar had given our city dwellers new hope. We had enjoyed the prominence. Who would not? And like superannuated prima donnas, we preserved the belief that we were still in the limelight; but now the signs of change were too many to be ignored. There was more doing than defence.

A November night and the following morning in 1942 were, to me, significant. We had a programme of trial flying which involved much scrutiny and peering between one aircraft and another; a cloudless sky would have been the best conditions for it. A gloomy weather forecaster gave a discouraging picture of the weather; the trials were in consequence cancelled and we went to the mess. It was at about eleven o'clock when I heard several aircraft going overhead; the noise soon increased to a thunder and then died away to the spasmodic outbreaks of the stragglers. A raid was going out in weather I had readily denounced as unfit for our trials. Local weather was then clear, and needing to restore our self-respect we reinstituted our programme and flew, but unsuccessfully.

I was lying in bed next morning half awake, feeling satisfied that we had in the end done all we could the night before. Suddenly I was jerked into full consciousness. There was an aircraft close and it sounded as if it was coming over the mess. I looked out of the window at a grey wall of drizzle, and cloud at 200 or

300 hundred feet. This was what our forecaster had seen ahead and had mistimed. It looked impossible for a stranger to land at Ford. The machine passed very close, and the noise of its four Merlins gave way momentarily to a swishing sound; it was very low.

The noise faded away. I suspected that he had had a shot at getting in and had given up, but I felt helplessly anxious, because I knew that a returning bomber could not have much petrol left and that a desperate effort to get down—an overwhelming tendency springing from more than a desire to save an aeroplane—could lead to disaster to the north where the Downs would certainly be in cloud. It came over again, and now I felt sure that it must be in difficulties. The noise died away and, as is often the case when one is powerless to help, I thought of other things for a bit, turned over and went to sleep again. I had ample excuse for being late. Had I not flown the night before?

At breakfast there was a stranger, and I sat down next to him and asked where he came from. He mentioned an airfield in Lincolnshire.

"Lancs?" I asked.

"Yes."

"When did you arrive here?"

"This morning."

"What was it like?"

"Not so easy. We were on instruments most of the way across France."

"Did you have any difficulty getting in here? I heard you come over the mess twice."

"No, not really. We made two bosh shots at it, but got in O.K. the third."

"Where did you go?"

"Turin."

"How long did it take?"

"About eight hours."

"What were the defences like?"

"They've increased. There are two guns now, and they must be manned by Germans because they went on firing after the bombs began to fall."

Targets were not often in Italy, and not all got off so lightly, even in those days. The bomber crews were going hard at it, several times a week, whenever the weather allowed, plugging away, making trips of six, eight or more hours, getting shot up and limping back with dead men on board, engines out or with no hydraulics, scrambling in, say to Ford, to feed and sleep and then to return to their station in Lincolnshire or Yorkshire to prepare for it all over again.

The case for our taking a small part in this offensive was strong. A new technique was being developed of catching the enemy fighter out in the dark, taking him on in his own air, pitting our wits, guided by radar and radio, against his; and this was appropriate to our rôle. It was a competition in radio design and performance, and we, an operational trials unit, could not be left out of it. The authorities relented and we were told to go ahead.

This was reinvigorating. At Ford it was more than just the news of casualties that made one want to have a go at the enemy fighters. The casualties and the battle damage were often there. Unforgettable was a Lancaster from whose mid-upper turret the headless corpse of the gunner had been removed the night before. It was gory and shocking; a cannon-shell had hit and burst in the turret, and the rest of the aircraft was riddled with jagged holes. Those chaps had had little chance. I was not alone in feeling a worm when I thought of the relative safety of our job.

Even one Mosquito fighter would help, since it might chase or be chased by an enemy fighter, and thus make him miss the opportunity of destroying a bomber; for our belief, which was exaggerated perhaps and would have been hotly contested by the bomber crews, was that once a fighter had made contact with a big bomber, the bomber was as good as destroyed. We who had never been up against more than one rear gun did not realise the effect on the enemy of four guns in a turret. From the enemy fighter crews themselves I was to hear later that it had been more than we had believed. Nevertheless, a bomber, and a big one at that, was at a fundamental disadvantage, which we understood far better than their crews. There was always the chance that a lone Mosquito, besides perhaps decoying and diverting an enemy fighter, might even catch one unawares. It was well worth trying.

Such an operation, though experimental in its equipment, would not of course be without precedent. Intruder fighters—first Blenheims, then Bostons and later Mosquitoes—had been operating for years past with marked success (which was surprisingly lasting), first against bombers and later against fighters near their own bases. Being without radar, these fighters had to depend for their interceptions on the enemy using navigation lights, and in this he obliged and continued to oblige, though to a diminishing extent, to the end.

A recent development, which was a pointer to the counter-offensive against the night-fighters, was the equipment of Beaufighters with an early type of radar, released for use in enemy air, and with a special radio outfit for receiving the enemy fighter radar frequencies. The latter indicated the enemy's direction and with it the course to steer to intercept. This operation with Beaufighters was initially a great success. The enemy's transmissions could be received and homed on from fifty miles away, and this range, and the fact that the reception of these transmissions immediately identified an aircraft as hostile, allowed the Beaufighters to pick the enemy fighters out of the myriads of bombers, the needles out of the haystack. Successes were frequent. Bob Braham,[1] the commanding officer of that squadron, scored particularly rapidly and brilliantly. He and Sticks Gregory[2] and Jacko,[3] his alternate observers, seemed to have taken the measure of the enemy fighters. By a combination of great radar operating, good team-work and Bob's ability to turn a Beaufighter tightly at night, they accounted for five or six in rapid succession.

In this, as in intruding—another homing operation —success depended upon transmissions from the aircraft to be intercepted. The enemy's radar transmissions were to these Beaufighters what his navigation lights were to the intruders. His presence was detected and his direction determined by this means; but his distance remained uncertain until either the

[1] Wing Commander J. R. D. Braham, D.S.O., D.F.C., A.F.C.
[2] Squadron Leader W. J. Gregory, D.S.O., D.F.C., D.F.M.
[3] Squadron Leader H. Jacobs, D.F.C., A.F.C.

intruder was able to distinguish and see the distance between the navigation lights or the Beaufighter observer got a radar contact. Homing was a neat operation, but its future was uncertain, since its success depended on the enemy's co-operation, and he might (but did not ever entirely) give up using navigation lights and use his radar intermittently and only when among the bombers (where he would be hard to single out).

Bob and several others had detected enemy fighters stealing up behind them (their radar had a short range rearwards), and while some of them had evaded and lost contact, others had turned the tables by a very quick turn, had got behind their opponent and had then attacked after a normal interception. These successes suggested that the enemy fighters could not 'see' radar-wise behind them, and so this manœuvre seemed promising.

These Beaufighters were potentially murderous weapons, but their duration did not allow them to go far or to patrol for long, and their radar range astern was poor. The Mosquito, not yet fitted with the homing gear, had speed at height and a longer duration, and if its radar coverage could be extended to the rear (a feasible modification), it would probably have a good chance of success even though it had no homing gear.

Our fighter radar installations, needing maximum range ahead, were naturally designed to transmit predominantly forward, and with their aerials so set out their range astern was poor. For defence this was acceptable, but the offensive fighter required also a view behind, sufficient both in range and coverage. The longer the rearward range the better, for the greater the distance at which the rapid turn to get behind the enemy was made, the less chance was there of its development being noticed soon enough for him to follow, and the greater the peace of mind of the crew. Frank Clarke,[1] our radar officer, reckoned that the addition of a second transmitter, feeding an aerial fitted inside the fuselage and directed rearwards, would give the desired result, the wooden fuselage reducing the effective range but little. He was allowed to make the installation in our Mosquito, and results were most promising. By switching the power from one transmitter to the other and using always the same receiver, the observer could have a quick look behind to a distance of about four miles and then, by switching over, look ahead again. With this, aircraft patrols of adequate duration became possible at distant target areas and at other points where concentrations of enemy fighters might be expected, and with this equipment an opponent approaching from behind or even crossing behind became as important as an opponent detected ahead; but the technique of the quick turn to get on his tail needed some working out and practice.

To prepare for operations over enemy territory, we began to practise the crude but effective navigation that sufficed for the intruders, flying low and picking a way by dead reckoning from landmark to landmark, from river bend to coastline or whatever feature showed up. Then, to get used to it, we did a trip over

[1] Flight Lieutenant F. C. Clarke, killed in action, November 26, 1943.

the Low Countries through the enemy fighter area. Next came the long wait for a turn to go out with the bombers.

Progress was slow. We had only one Mosquito suitable for these operations, and it was so damaged in a heavy landing one night that we had to start again from the beginning and modify a replacement machine; but we clung to the first when it had been repaired and, though it was surplus to our establishment, Hicko contrived that we should keep it. Thus we had two aircraft, and the time came at last when we were all ready to operate in support of the bombers.

My turn came round, and one September evening Frank and I were at a Suffolk airfield for briefing on the bomber plan. Frank, the unit's radar specialist, was part creator of our new installation and, having an insatiable passion for flying, he had leapt at the suggestion of coming with me; having flown a lot together, we knew each other's ways, and I was confident that he would navigate me safely, and that when we met the enemy he would exploit the new gear to the full, giving me the best chance to make an effective contribution, and enabling me ultimately to play successfully the pilot's only solo part in these interceptions—the approach and attack. At that airfield we joined a small number of crews from certain defensive squadrons which still had the older type of radar; they, too, were being allowed with it over enemy territory, with the hope of at least decoying and at most destroying enemy fighters.

We were not due off till after dark and with time in hand we had supper (for which I had little appetite) and went into the mess garden. It was the end of a perfect day; except for the birds, all was still, and in the east the blue of the sky was just darkening. Such perfect tranquillity contrasted with my thoughts. How grotesque it was that we now had to go out to fly for hundreds of miles over territory whose masters would be intent on our destruction as soon as they became aware of our presence; it was in one way the last thing that I wanted to do.

The noise of an aircraft broke in on this unsettling reverie. It grew and multiplied, and as soon as eyes got the range, little black shapes became visible, high up and right overhead, perhaps at 10,000 feet, all moving relentlessly eastward towards the German city chosen for that night's target. The commotion spread till the air reverberated with a steady far-away thunder. The sky seemed full. There were hundreds and some were making vapour trails. I remembered the raid on Coventry. The bombers had come over our airfield, not in a mass as these, but singly. There had not been this vibrating firmament-filling din, but instead an uneven and fluctuating throbbing which rose and died away, to recur with Prussian regularity as another raider passed unscathed. Then—it seemed long ago—we had been grounded by weather, frustrated and wholly ineffective.

Someone exclaimed: "Crikey, look at that! One's on fire." I swung round and, looking to where he was pointing, saw a Stirling with a plume of smoke coming from it. A bad oil leak was my first thought, but as I looked a small glow appeared near its tail and increased steadily, as when an ember is fanned. The

'The sky seemed full.' A raid going out at dusk

Imperial War Museum Photograph

The Author

(From the portrait owned by Sheffield City Art Galleries)

Wing Commander G. C. Maxwell,

M.C., D.F.C., A.F.C.

machine flew on steadily and there were no parachutes. So deliberate was the development of this disaster, as seen from the ground, that momentarily I thought the crew must have the situation under control. But then things happened with sickening swiftness. A gentle dive started, seemingly still under control, but as we watched the fire grew and spread, enveloping the whole tail; the dive steepened and quickened, becoming nearly vertical; there was an explosion which broke the machine into two pieces; and so it disappeared from view. Another explosion some minutes later told us that the bombs had gone off, and we realised that here was a mystery that would never be solved, for there could have been no survivors.

In those days the briefing of the few free-lance fighter crews on the bomber plan was somewhat rudimentary, and that night there were also delays which caused us to take off late. We learnt that the target was Hanover, and we realised that our only plan then must be to go straight there; for although the attack would probably be over by the time we arrived, there would be a chance of meeting fighters which were staying after the raid's end to catch the stragglers. We went off hurriedly. Half-way across the North Sea all the radar broke down and we knew then that we could only be spectators; but we needed experience, and after a moment's thought we went on. From the Dutch coast we could see flak and searchlights in the distance, and soon we saw fires ahead. I began to wonder whether the unique chance might once more be presented; we needed great luck, but if we had it—and I had had it before—we might see an enemy fighter in the light of the fires or even one burning navigation lights.

It seemed to take no time and soon we were over the target. Here, so I thought as we circled high above, was a whole town on fire. The extent of the fires was scarcely credible, and over them the impression of height was falsified. Had I had no altimeter I would have guessed we were at 2,000 and not 16,000 feet. This conflagration was much bigger than any I had seen in our cities. I was to discover some months later from photographs and reports that the city had hardly been hit in this raid and that most of the bombs had fallen in woods outside. Nevertheless, this was awe-inspiring and, sight-seeing in relative security, I thought of the mad drama of it all; for here in the night sky over this city had been the site of a contest between every means of offence and defence that the best brains could devise and the greatest factories produce; here that night they had been pitted against each other, and the result was the acres of fire below.

Of the enemy fighters we saw only pyrotechnic recognition signals, and we knew our chances of visual contact were all but nil. They were there all right, but without radar we were blind. Had we wanted proof that a fighter without radar was useless in this kind of situation, here it was.

I remembered motoring through Hanover in 1938 soon after the Munich Crisis. I had had to stop to ask the way. I spoke to a young officer, and he answered civilly, offering to come with me to put me on the right road, an offer I readily accepted. He directed me efficiently and in monosyllables; he refused to be drawn into conversation and, having shown me the main road, he got out and saluted smartly. He must have realised the gravity of the crisis just passed, and I, a near-enemy alien, had to be treated no more than correctly. Idly I wondered what had become of him now; probably he had died somewhere for Hitler.

The return to Ford was uneventful, and we landed there four hours after take-off. With no radar and only short-range radio, there were occasional sneaking anxieties; but home is a big objective from a few hundred miles away, and from a fix we were able to make just before crossing the coast we found ourselves not far off track. This trip had not been entirely fruitless.

As time went on we were able to send out one or two Mosquitoes every night the bombers went out. According to the distance of the bomber's target, they flew either to the enemy fighters' supposed marshalling points or along the flank of the bomber 'stream' and so to the target, where they stayed until the bomber concentration was lessening; and where enemy fighters, uncertain whether the attack was over, would also remain. Results, though encouraging, were confusing. There had been many—if anything, too many—radar contacts with aircraft many of which must have been hostile, but the contacts had been inconclusive. Soon, however, a squadron crew, by following a random contact near Berlin, showed what could be done and destroyed a Me.110. This raised our hopes.

Then one night Bob [1] and Staggers,[2] members of our naval counterpart unit, went missing. Although

[1] Lieutenant Commander H. R. Spedding, R.N.
[2] Lieutenant Commander G. S. Staveley, R.N.V.R.

the crews of this unit worked primarily on naval interception problems, with naval aircraft and equipment,
they also flew R.A.F. aircraft in trials and operations,
and so it happened that Bob and Staggers were bound
for the bombers' target in a R.A.F. Mosquito. The
weather was bad over the south coast, but it improved
along the route, and although our second machine returned early with reports of heavy icing, we assumed
that Bob and Staggers had got through this patch of
bad weather and were well on their way with the
bombers. Yet I could not be sure. Conditions sounded
bad for their climb away from Ford, and I thought of
all that might have gone wrong, the failure of their
radio or an engine, and a forced landing at some other
airfield. Our weather was hardly fit for a return on
one engine; it was, in fact, bad enough to cause a
panicky pilot from one squadron to land in a deluge
of rain on a decoy airfield a few miles away from Ford.

I had to go to a party at a small mess in Bognor, but
with this anxiety I left early and went to the flight
office. The naval van was there standing outside, as it
had been left; they had not landed. We went to the
mess and waited for news, but there was no news.
What happened regularly among the bomber crews
was new to us. The realisation at last that they could
no longer be airborne was like a hit in the face; they
must be down somehow, somewhere. There was nothing to be done, and although we pretended to have
hope, we believed that they had 'had it'; there was no
point in losing any more sleep, and I went to bed.

In the early hours a message came with Bob's telephone number. He lived out and his wife would be

anxiously awaiting his return. There was no news; they had not come down in this country and were now officially missing. I had to break this news at once. I telephoned and, trying to conceal my own apprehensions, I said that Bob had not come back, that he had been heading for the bombers' target, but that we had, and she must have, hope; and she took it bravely. At the end of that conversation I had persuaded myself that the fact that they were missing did not mean that they were dead, and temporarily I was confident that they were safe; but as time passed without news the conviction prevailed that we would not see them again. The absence of two such popular figures was very depressing.

Bob and Staggers were not dead, and we saw them again more than eighteen months later, the former having been a prisoner and the latter a 'maquisard'. Theirs was another story of mistaken identity, for they had been shot down by another Mosquito which itself crashed, damaged by debris, its crew being made prisoners. Bob and Staggers were picked up by our fighter-control stations as they were crossing the Channel and, being unidentified, were plotted as a 'bogey'; there had been reports of enemy activity and a fighter was sent to investigate. It had some difficulty in overhauling this suspicious lone aircraft making for France, but succeeded at last in getting a long-range contact. What followed I can easily imagine. Overhauling slowly and out of touch with the ground station, the second Mosquito closes in; the pilot sees his quarry. Perhaps this is his first sight of what he believes to be an enemy aircraft, his first chance, as he

thinks, of shooting one down, a chance not to be missed
at any cost. However far over France he may be, his
infringement of regulations will surely be overlooked
if he is successful. It is obviously, he thinks, a Me.410.
He closes in and opens fire. There are hits on an
engine; pieces come off and the aircraft suddenly
slows down; he is overtaking alarmingly and there is
nothing he can do to avoid a glancing blow from the
wreckage; his aircraft becomes uncontrollable and he
and his observer bale out. They are picked up and a
few days later they meet Bob, the pilot of the aircraft
they had destroyed, also a P.o.W.

Chapter 14

SWANSONG

NIGHT flying never palled for me, and even after many hundreds of hours of it every sortie was fresh and vivid. There was much during those hours spent between heaven and earth to excite the imagination: the grim objective, the isolation and remoteness, the impression of being in some way detached from earthly ties, and the incomparable beauty of the scene —provided always that the weather had been left below. And as the curtain went up one might feel some exaltation, for as the aircraft charged down the lighted runway one knew that there was no going back; bound irrevocably for the dark unknown, unable now to alter things, one was resigned and contented; and as the curtain fell there was the fascination of a game of skill (a well-executed approach and landing needed good co-ordination of mind and muscle) with the delicious aftermath of relief and satisfaction, a duty accomplished. So it was that the flying in the late autumn of 1943, although much of it would have been unremarkable for some, was impressive for me, and it was especially significant because it marked the end of a phase; I had learnt that I was soon to be posted.

There was a fruitless forty-minute chase in cloud which ended somewhere over Norfolk. It was raining hard as we took off and cloud was unbroken up to more than 20,000 feet. George Cook [1] soon got a contact, but the enemy seemed to be aware of the pursuit and eventually we lost him. I recall the unsteadiness of my flying, George's skill and patience, and the iced-up windscreen. We got out of cloud at 23,000 feet, and after some delay re-established touch with the ground; we were directed towards Ford.

Still above cloud and at 20,000 feet, we were told that we were approaching Ford, and we left the starlit splendour for weird, electric and bumpy murk five miles deep. It was rough, perhaps rougher than I had ever known it. The Mosquito shook like a speedboat being driven over choppy seas; the electric discharges danced incessantly, first from side to side and then, as incomprehensible variations, from top to bottom of the windscreen, and finally they took the form of droplets impinging on it; there was a ghostly glow in the cockpit. The bacon-and-egg supper that rewarded the night fliers seemed very remote. So to lose 20,000 feet when one is scared and intent on a cautious descent takes time, but at last, with the altimeter showing about 1,500 feet, I saw some lights which though blurred and unintelligible showed me that we had broken cloud. As the ice on the windscreen dispersed, they took coherent shape and I recognised the familiar layout of Ford. We circled to let the ice clear and landed.

And as a contrast were anti-fighter-bomber patrols over London in the only radar Typhoon, for which the weather had to be clear. The western sky was still light when, after a novel and exciting take-off, I headed for

[1] Squadron Leader G. B. Cook, D.F.C.

London, climbing hard. That scene is unforgettable; it was, I thought, for me alone. London's outline was plain at first, and then, as the sun disappeared, it became dim, melted and vanished. I watched the sensational change from day to night, and as the sky changed from blue to starry-black, the city below, though blacked out, began to sparkle vulnerably with flashes from electric railways, a target impossible to miss. Sometimes I could forget my concern about the one engine which was keeping me airborne. It became complete night and a moon came up, making the fragments of cloud below give misleading impressions of the shape of the river. There was no sign of opponents; an hour passed and the time came for a return to base, an exhilarating dive towards Ford, followed within fifteen minutes by the landing, an operation embarrassed by a frosted windscreen and by the aircraft's nose which, once it came up, completely shut off the view ahead.

It was now official; I was to be posted to a staff job, and although this news was saddening it was perhaps timely—or so I felt when I realised that I was becoming nervous of flying in the dark. Yet this had happened before and, remembering its cure, I was not convinced that I needed a change. For a short time I joined John Cunningham in operating from West Malling on a special anti-fighter-bomber plan. Our war for the night was soon over, and then the importance of getting back to Ford and my own bed became paramount and I left for home. Once I left when fog had already formed, and a blind take-off, though no great feat in a Mosquito, called for concentration on and trust in instruments, obedience to rules, and a brief extra stressing of the nerves, which together provided the required remedy, short-lived though the effect might have been. I got back to normal.

My posting came through and I began to hand over to Chris Hartley.[1] I went to Fighter Command to see Hicko and find out about my future, but our talk was cut short by the news that a raid was planned for that night. I had been standing by for many nights past to accompany one; it was my turn, and this was my last chance of taking it, so I called up Ford, told them I wanted the one suitable Mosquito, passed the word to Frank Clarke, who was again coming as my radar-operator-navigator, and left the headquarters in a hurry.

There was no time to think of anything but immediate preparations; we had tea, dressed, were briefed, worked out our navigational plan, tested our aircraft and its equipment and took off; then suddenly there was no more haste. The curtain had come down on the scene of bustle and urgent activity. Climbing gently, we set course at just about the time when city offices were emptying and drawn, haggard, worried people were shoving and scrambling for buses and trains. Flying roughly south-east, we could see our own coast clearly as we crossed it; the Channel we could see hazily and the French coast not at all. A strange contentment reigned. Strapped in this little wooden box of a cockpit, immobile as a baby newly tucked up in its cot, I found a comforting inevitability in this sort of adventure. The issues were clear-cut and

[1] Group Captain C. H. Hartley, O.B.E., D.F.C., A.F.C.

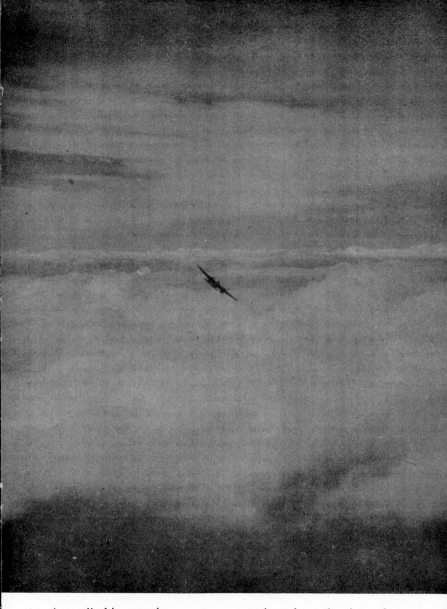

'. . . climbing gently we set course at just about the time when
city offices were emptying . . .'

'. . . I watched the departure one night of a Station's force of thirty Lancasters' (*See p.* 160)

initially I was not even scared. We were part of the night sky, or so we gladly felt, considering the hostility of the continent 20,000 feet below, and so we hoped to remain until we had recrossed our coast and regained the land. Creeping airborne across the face of Europe, four miles from the earth and at four to five miles per minute, we became different from the persons we were on land. Perhaps this was because height, our third dimension, ruled out that usual solution to most trouble—'get out and walk'. There were two targets that night, and it was on the southern one, Mannheim, that our plan was based. It was known that the opposing fighters used radio beacons as marshalling points and that, ordered off on the first alert, they stayed there until the bombers' intentions became clearer, when they were directed towards the target. Our plan was to go early to one of these likely points of congregation with the hope of running into a number of unsuspecting opponents. There would be little doubt of the nature of the aircraft found, and with our radar 'looking' both ahead and astern, we had hopes of finding them up to four miles ahead and three astern. We believed that our radar 'sight' was better than theirs.

We had taken off after the passage of the bombers, but flying much faster we soon began to overtake them, an invisible fleet several hundred strong heading south-east, unseen save as multiple blips on the radar tubes, each machine carrying seven young men, every one of them a volunteer, selected and highly trained for a demanding task, every one bringing part of his own world along with him, his own thoughts, his own

COVER OF DARKNESS

hopes and his own anxieties. And suddenly we were
reminded that we were in enemy air. A machine
caught fire and, seen only as a ball of flame, fell with
a sickening slowness and exploded on hitting the
ground. Perhaps a fighter guided by a wide-awake
controller had got there early and had scored, just as
we had done on occasion over the Channel two years
before. Tensed, our complacency shaken, we expected
something else to happen, we knew not what; but it
did not happen, and all went on as before and the
burning aircraft was left behind, a beacon, not far
from Amiens.

The bombers, too, were left behind, and our radar
was 'seeing' nothing. We were in haze, and though we
climbed to 25,000 feet, it persisted. So we had to
continue at that height, the pilot doing his best, more
on instruments than he liked, to fly with an accuracy
that would give some chance of success in the somewhat exacting plan of reaching the near vicinity of a
radio beacon several hundred miles away without that
beacon's aid.

Pilots' aptitudes for instrument flying must vary, as
do temperaments, and little is known by pilots of each
other's abilities or difficulties in the air beyond what
they themselves choose to say. Tests in a Link trainer
can give an idea of the speed of a pilot's reaction and
his knowledge of procedures, but his true flying ability
is usually known only to himself and he is the only
judge of the effort needed to produce the result. Yet
the ultimate result is there for all to see if he survives,
since survival shows, if nothing else, an average competence. An average competence was all I could claim,

150

and I never knew how I stood relative to others. I used to feel that I was as good as those who were honest and admitted difficulties, better than those who bragged about the way they took it all in their stride, tight turns in the dark and all, and far below the experts who said little, who survived and who had temperaments of the right sort. Perhaps I was good at blind-flying, perhaps I was bad at it; but most probably I was just average, and that implied that a short spell was all right, more was a bore, and a lot was hell. This night it was a bore, for excepting the haze the weather was fine.

After an hour my contentment had disappeared and I was feeling queasy. There was a long way to go to get home, and the ground was very hostile. The sudden appearance of searchlights on a cloud below reminded us forcibly of this, and we made several rapid alterations of course. After waving about, it seemed aimlessly, the searchlights went out as suddenly as they had come on, and we were left again decently in a darkness that was complete except for the sickly green of the cathode-ray tubes and the fluorescence of the engine and flying instruments. Our passage had been noticed, but we would probably be ignored. What did one aircraft matter to the enemy out of more than a thousand?

At eight minutes past eight, two hours after taking off from Ford, we should have reached the beacon, but we saw and found nothing. We began a square search, flying five-minute legs, but still there was nothing but a few tiny lights on the ground. The chances of meeting the enemy had not been good. The beacon idea was a gamble both in time and place, with the added uncertainty of the navigation factor; we were not surprised to find ourselves with that large block of enemy air all to ourselves. We wasted no more time and set course from that hypothetical point to the target, in which plan there would be fewer uncertainties. The time and the place would be certain, and once the attack had started there would be no navigation factor, because it would be seen from a great distance. Over the target the uncertainty, as had already been well proven by many crews, was the identity of the aircraft intercepted; there were many bombers to each fighter, and the problem was to pick the Luftwaffe needles out of the R.A.F. haystack when time was short. Aircraft there were, hundreds of them, but interception after interception had ended abortively with the sight of a bomber.

We were going to arrive late, some twenty minutes or so after the end of the attack, but the enemy did not know its duration and their fighters might be kept in the neighbourhood after the departure of the bombers, or might arrive late as we were doing.

It should have taken us seventeen minutes. Fifteen minutes passed and we saw nothing. Where were we? This was the dominant among many unsettling thoughts. We were caught, held and lost by searchlights. Seventeen minutes passed and, as we were beginning to wonder whether it was possible for us to be so far off track as to miss the target altogether, I noticed a glimmer well over to port, a light of sorts. A moment later we came into clearer air, and the light grew and we could see luminescence on the clouds.

This must be the target. We were miles off track. We turned towards it, and after what seemed an age the whole staggering sight was below us. Through holes, as it were, torn in the cloud and lit up by the glare below, we could see a city on fire. The streets were outlined by flame just as Plymouth's streets had been, and fires seemed to have taken a hold everywhere. It was more than half an hour after zero hour and the bombers should by then have been on the homeward route, but it was worth a try and we started to patrol across the bombing run.

Frank suddenly reported a big aircraft crossing above us. We turned and closed in till we were less than 300 yards away below (from where a Lancaster should have been easily seen), but I could see nothing, and I broke away for fear that, seen by an alert gunner, we would get a hail of bullets in our faces. I tried coming in again, but again unaccountably we had no success and we began to doubt the radar—it had probably saved a JU 88 from destruction over the North Sea nearly two years before. Then, talking as quickly as he could, Frank said dramatically:

"I've got something else coming in behind from the left, coming up fast—wait, wait—now, turn hard left."

I turned as hard as I could. Our radar showed that he was after us and initially I thought only of saving my skin. I was trying to outmanœuvre him so as to come up behind, where his radar was (so we believed) blind. In this sort of a competition the Mosquito was a match for most of the German fighters, and our radar equipment made a surprise attack impossible. We were in fact very secure; but the idea of an enemy fighter coming up behind frightened me enough to make me tighten the turn as much as I dared, the whole machine shuddering now and again, and to force me to depend completely on Frank's commentary.

"I've still got it. Go on turning."

And on we went, milling round with our invisible opponent following, we construed, in circles too. How odd this blind-man's buff would have looked in daylight to a spectator in a balloon. He would have seen two aircraft doing steep turns in the vicinity of each other with no apparent aim. Yet had he seen inside them and had he been able to overhear what was passing between the observers and their pilots, he would have realised that this was a tense competition. He would have seen the observers with their heads hard up against the visors of their radar sets, doing all they could to interpret to their pilots the crude signs denoting what their aircraft's eye was seeing. Perhaps one of them was cursing the inadequacy of his gear. The spectator would have seen one aircraft stop turning.

"He's ahead now, I think. Stop turning."

"Steady. That's fine. He's 2,000 feet away."

The observer in the balloon would have seen that the second aircraft had unaccountably stopped turning too; it was astern of the first.

"You're closing up well; he's 1,500 feet away, ahead and above."

"Throttle back a bit."

"Twelve hundred feet, forty-five degrees up, dead ahead."

"I think I can see his exhausts. Carry on."

The second aircraft would have been seen closing up slowly in line astern formation on the first; it would have looked very normal.

"Eight hundred [feet]."

"Six hundred."

"Yes. That's it. Have a look."

"It's a 110. You must watch this."

By now we had closed right up, and then fell back slowly as we came up level. And now the spectator in the balloon would have learnt what it was all about, even though he could not understand why it had had to be done in that way. I opened fire from about a hundred yards and hits registered immediately on that luckless aircraft; there was a vivid flash and I had to pause to take aim again. I fired again and there were more flashes; my windscreen became momentarily obscured by some liquid that came back at us and he turned and dived away. Circling slowly I saw against the blackness of the ground what might have been a catherine wheel close to us. How far away it was I could not tell in the dark, but a moment later it hit the ground and exploded.

After waiting ten more minutes in the target area, expecting to find another opponent, we set course for home. As we left that eerie scene our impression was that the enemy knew it was all over too, and was concentrating only on getting his fighters down. Searchlights were now only homing and an airfield was seen fully lit up. There would have been opportunities there, but after weighing them up we ignored them. Our radar was of very little use at low altitude, its range being dependent on height, and it would have taken ten to fifteen minutes to clear from the windscreen the moisture that always formed during rapid descent. It was not worthwhile, and reluctantly we left, knowing that we had a comfortable margin. The return was as uneventful as it was jubilant, and we landed at Ford at five minutes to eleven, four and three-quarter hours after we had left.

Chapter 15

BOMBER COMMAND

I WAS posted to Bomber Command, to a radio counter-measures Group which had yet to be formed.
My new A.O.C. gave me a day off-duty and told me
to meet him at Command Headquarters.

To me Bomber Command was new in outlook, new
in machinery of command, new in conception of planning and new in people. Now senior R.A.F. partner in
the air war, representing, so it was said, a share of
the nation's effort which would have equipped and
kept going twenty-five divisions of troops, Bomber
Command was profoundly impressive. It was all
new. There was not the spur-of-the-moment action of
fighter operations. Instead there was an almost ponderous deliberation. The initiative was theirs and
command was centralised. At a planning conference,
which had an air of ceremony, the Commander-in-
Chief chose the target and laid down the scale of
attack, and later, when there was any doubt, he made
the final decision as to whether or not the plan should
go through. The force he controlled was spread over
a large part of England, and at that time it could
muster in an operation more than a thousand aircraft.

The Command was proud and defiant. Losses of
thirty, forty or more aircraft per night, though tragic
in individual thought and seemingly crippling to the
newcomer, were accepted by the Command as a whole

stoically and unflinchingly. Ranks were filled by the products of a vast training and industrial effort. New crews were ready to move into the front line and new aircraft were ready for them to fly; the battle was maintained. Bomber Command's war never flagged; it had been going on since the beginning, and our ejection from France had been the signal for its building to the present scale. Bombing under cover of the dark remained the only way in which we could hit the enemy from this country, and there had been no let-up. Bomber Command had good reason to be proud.

I was an unobtrusive witness of the planning conference, and when the C.-in-C. had withdrawn from the sanctuary-like atmosphere of the operations-room, I saw the building and learned the details of a plan for an attack which required the arrival over a distant target, on that self-same night, of more than a thousand bombers within fifteen minutes or less. I was becoming acquainted with a part of the Air Force which had hitherto been remote.

Visits to Group headquarters and bomber stations conveyed more of the size of the Command than did the order of battle in the operations-room at the Command headquarters, and I began to understand now why it was that the frequent losses of thirty or more bombers, when spread over the many squadrons that made up the Command, were not crippling. Considerate staff officers explained to me the more detailed Group plan for an attack on Berlin, and at a station of that Group I attended a briefing on the plan. A whistle, half in protest and half in jest, went up as the curtain was drawn aside, revealing to the crews the night's target and their route. I looked at those intent faces. They were ordinary-looking men. They must have come from all sorts of families and homes and have been to all sorts of schools, a group typical, I thought, of the Service. In these highly trained crews brain was more important than muscle, and they were as expendable as the infantry of the first war; these men, too, had to 'go over the top', and it happened several times a week. Was this, I have since wondered, the end of a phase in warfare, the high-water mark in wastage restricted to experts?

Did they realise how small were their chances if once seen by a fighter? I guessed that none knew that the exhausts of their Lancasters could be spotted from a mile and a half, and that they could be seen as silhouettes against the stars from nearly a mile away, while the fighter could be seen against the ground at only about a hundred yards. These were grim thoughts, and knowing full well the theoretical bias against the big bomber, I hoped that the facts would never be known by the crews, but would become more and more dominant in the moulding of tactics and the trend of planning. My feelings towards these men were of simple admiration, and later, when I had heard stories of the occasional superstitions which gave to some of them comfort and a feeling of greater security —a pilot's lucky pair of boots, the whip which another cracked before and after each operation, and the suicidal speciality of a third of flying well away from the bomber stream in which all the fighters were believed to be—my admiration was tinged with a mixture of sadness, pity and sentiment which is hard to describe.

Standing near the marshalling point I watched the departure one night of a station's force of thirty Lancasters. Each machine took up its position on the runway; each engine was run up with a thunder that shook the ground and, while final checks were made, Waafs standing near waved to friends among the crews who, helmeted, masked and confined in perspex cages, responded with a supremely confident thumbs-up fist. Throttles were opened wide, brakes were released and, in a great commotion, the first machine rolled off, the gunner perhaps dipping his guns in salutation. Gathering speed rapidly, it receded into the gloom and left the earth, disappearing momentarily, to reappear, as it climbed, against the last light of day. As one bomber was airborne another was there, ready to go. The departure of this force took little more than forty minutes, and then I was taken to the station-commander's house for a drink and dinner in comfort. That particular night—the target was not Berlin—thirty came back to that station, and all but two were down within forty-five minutes without trouble. This was no stunt, but a miracle of organisation and drill which happened regularly; it was, one felt, an ultimate performance like the highest high jump. It might be bettered, but the margins would be fractional only.

To add to the staff officer's picture of the Berlin raid, I visited the station where German radio was intercepted, and there I was able to listen to some of the enemy fighter-controller's orders and to get an idea of the reaction to the raid. Very early on all fighters were sent to Berlin, and I knew that some of those men I had seen at the briefing would soon be up against it. The German controller sounded calm and unhurried as he repeated mechanically with much guttural rolling of the R's, "Alle Dromedär-r-re nach Bär-r-e"—Dromedäre being the call sign of a certain group of squadrons and Bäre being their code name for Berlin. My blood ran cold; this was gruesome and depressing. The enemy would be waiting there in hordes, and I believed there would be disastrous losses.

The broadcasting from this station of bogus instructions to enemy fighters, of reports of deterioration of weather and orders to land, had started some little time before and had been an immediate success. Confirmation of the success of this subterfuge came from the enemy controllers themselves, who became angry and as abusive as fishwives; they were answered back and, had it been possible to feel sorry for Nazis, one would have felt sorry for those fighter crews who had to listen.

That night our 'spoof' was moderately successful. A bogus order from us was countered by the German controller telling his crews not to listen to the Englishman; the latter then countered by an almost word-perfect repetition of those instructions. Identities became confused after a few such exchanges and, to annoy and upset the crews and further to add to the confusion, our broadcaster began an impassioned impersonation of Hitler. The tension broke and we laughed heartily.

COVER OF DARKNESS

Losses that night could not be called disastrous. Forty for Berlin was reckoned average. Bomber Command could take these losses. Other crews and other aircraft would be there to take-off the next night.

Chapter 16

R.C.M.

AT a R.A.F. headquarters at Radlett the Group acquired an office and a telephone. This was our base for the first week and here my A.O.C. left messages for me and I for him. A corporal, W.A.A.F., arrived and the first simple organisation started to work. She answered the telephone, reported our whereabouts, took messages and typed spasmodically.

Quickly armed with an establishment, we began to look for staff. Priority was high and we were helped unstintingly in our search. We visited units and stations which were to come into the Group, and in the course of several long motor journeys which these visits entailed, we talked about the difficulties ahead and, what was for me a mystery—radio warfare. Bit by bit I learnt of our radio counter-measure defence against the blitz of 1940–41 which, under the A.O.C.'s command, had done amongst other things what the public called 'bending the beam'.

This story has been told, but an outline, constructed for myself as a layman from what I learnt then and in the ensuing eighteen engrossing and vivid months, is appropriate to any story of radio counter-measures, for the radio war began, not in 1943, but in the black days of 1940–41, when I was a fighter pilot, living from day to day, not worrying much about the war in general and supremely content in my own little world.

During those critical days, when the war was near to being lost and the Nazi's well-planned and furious onslaught was at its height, an organisation was built up almost overnight which interfered so seriously with the Luftwaffe's radio bombing-aids as to discredit them and to enforce a major change in technique.

The enemy began bombing us at night with the use of radio beams to guide his bombers to their targets. From stations on the German, Dutch, Belgian and French coasts a suitable pair of beams was trained to intersect over the chosen target, and the bombers, using their ordinary beam receivers, flew along the one beam until they heard the other and so knew that they were near the target. The raid could not be concentrated, but every bomber could find the target, provided always that the beams were dependable. This system scored some major successes for the enemy, among which the destruction of the centre of Coventry will probably be remembered longest. We were unprepared; our fighter defence, as has already been recounted, was not yet on its feet, and thus at the outset we were virtually defenceless. It was indeed fortunate for us that this secret weapon was susceptible to interference and that an effective counter-measure organisation was set up in such a short time. Had the enemy been able to use beam bombing unhindered, all our major industrial and transport centres would have been hit as Coventry was.

What, in simple terms, is a radio beam? The answer to this question needs to be known if this, the opening round of the radio war, is to be understood. A radio beam is analogous to two parallel and slightly overlapping searchlight beams. A man walking across the path of these two beams would be illuminated by one, then by both and then by the second. If the search-lights were transmitting not light but radio waves, and if the man had a radio receiver tuned to them, he would hear one, then both and then the second, as he moved across their path. Suppose that the first was turned on for a short period and turned off for a long period, while the other was on during that same long period and off for the short period—that the trans-missions were in fact of interlocking dots and dashes —then the observer crossing the paths would hear first dots, next a constant note and finally dashes; and by contriving always to hear a constant note he would be following the path of what is known as a radio beam. Properly directed, this beam could provide a pre-determined track to a target.

R.C.M. began by using radio-therapy apparatus taken from hospitals, not, as was the common belief, on account of the help it might give the bombers, but because it was the only apparatus available which could in any way interfere with the beams. It was re-installed in certain key targets, and was turned on when the beams were laid on them. Ground listening stations were opened to watch constantly for the beams, and their detection became the signal for the despatch of aircraft fitted with the necessary radio receivers to find and fly down them, thus detecting the enemy's target intentions early.

Special gear for transmitting dots or dashes on the beam frequencies was designed, manufactured and installed at strategic positions. It could produce spurious constant notes in a nearby beam, and the bomber pilot, hearing a constant note composed of enemy dots and our dashes, or vice-versa, would wrongly believe himself to be on the beam. Known to the public as bending the beam, this counter-measure was sometimes highly successful, and it led to a general discrediting of bombing on these beams. To make beam flying more unpopular, it 'leaked' out that our fighters had been equipped with beam receivers and were flying down the beams. Reacting to this, the enemy pilots would tend to fly in dots or dashes, just out of the constant-note path, and so were more easily led up the garden path on a bogus beam.

Other enemy navigational aids were likewise attacked. Radio beacons were listened for and their signals automatically re-transmitted at high power. Thus two signals, one probably from France and the other from England, would be heard by the enemy radio operators as one signal from somewhere in between (for the time interval between reception of the two signals would be so short as to pass unnoticed); and so beacons, too, were brought into some disrepute.

The reaction to all this was the adoption of path-finder tactics by the enemy, a special force going ahead with incendiaries to find the target by one or other highly specialised method, and to start fires as guides for the following forces. As one counter-measure, while efforts were made to extinguish these fires quickly, a realistic decoy fire would be lit some distance from the threatened city. There could be no relaxing. As soon as one navigation or bombing system had been countered, one or more others, probably more com-

plex and harder to interfere with, would be introduced
—and they too had to be identified, nailed down and
rendered useless to the enemy.

Besides spoiling bombing accuracy, these early counter-measures sometimes led to the complete undoing
of a crew. The Junkers 88 I saw on an unfinished airfield in Somerset in the autumn of 1941 had been
flown by such a crew. The machine had landed that
morning, the pilot believing he was somewhere in
France. It was said that the crew were arguing hotly
as they tumbled, cold and cramped, out of the kennel-
sized Ju.88 cockpit to discover their mistake. During
one of our motor journeys I learnt from the A.O.C.
that this bomber, one of the last over the country, had
been given the undivided attention of the radio counter-measure organisation. It was plotted coming south,
and was then seen to wander off, as it received false
beacon bearings. Then our beacon transmissions were
turned off and, receiving true bearings, it turned south
again. It was given more of this treatment with variations, and was soon hopelessly lost. One can imagine
what was going on in that small cockpit. Which bearing was right? Were any right? What did the navigator think? What did the pilot think? Perhaps they
had gone too far. Better go back north a bit. Try
again; and perhaps this time the beacon bearings were
true for a short time, but not for long. All the time the
aircraft was being plotted by our Observer Corps; all
the time the annoyance and mutual distrust in that
cramped cockpit must have been growing. And so this
tragi-comedy went on to its finale, when in a misty
dawn the pilot, insisting that the Severn was the Eng-

lish Channel, landed at the first airfield he saw.

Since 1941, when we had used radio counter-measures against bombing, the need for them had spread on land and sea and in the air wherever the enemy's use of radio waves could be interfered with, could give information or could be used otherwise to our advantage, and this led to the formation of our Group with the rôle of providing counter-measures how, where and when they were required. The Group was established in Bomber Command, whose need for R.C.M. was acute and continuous. This narrative is only concerned with the support given to the bombers.

As was to be expected, the effectiveness of the cover of the dark was decreasing, and in 1943 fighters were finding our bombers. Night had begun to be turned into day and bomber losses had become serious. Once the enemy had established an efficient fighter-control system, the scales were weighted heavily against the bombers, for aircraft once seen were vulnerable at night, the light always allowing an approach and attack as if 'out of the sun'; and even were other things equal, the big bombers could, because of their size, be seen before the small fighters. So the fighter could shoot first and, with its heavier armament, perhaps decisively, while the bomber's only sure safeguard (other than the use of an effective warning device) was constant evasive action, which would certainly hinder the fighter-pilot's aim and might even deny him a sighting. But the bombers flew in high concentration, timing had to be precise and navigation accurate, and these prerequisites were not compatible with much evasive action. Thus extraordinary measures had had to be adopted, and were now to be strengthened, to interfere with the enemy defences and so reduce the number of sightings by their fighters.

Each link in the fighter system was vulnerable to R.C.M., the early warning radar (the long-range 'sight'), the fighter controlling radar (the contact giver to the fighter's radar), the fighter's own radar which gave the sighting, and the vital channel of communication between the controller and the fighter. These links, and also the A.A. gun ranging and laying radar, were susceptible, and each needed separate treatment.

R.C.M. has two general forms—exploitation, and interference or jamming. Mention has already been made of the exploitation of enemy signals, the listening to fighter instructions and the broadcasting of false ones, the homing on enemy fighters and, in our own defence, the beam 'bending'; it tended to make the use of the enemy's radio and radar equipment undependable and even dangerous, and its ultimate result, though not always its aim, might be to condemn the enemy's equipment to disrepute and disuse.

Interference or jamming was less subtle, being designed to confuse or obliterate. A homely everyday example is the effect on radio reception of nearby unscreened electric machines (a lift, an electric razor or a passing car) or another broadcast station on or near the same wavelength. Then the announcer's speech can be obliterated or so confused as to become unintelligible. In the radio war the fighter controller was the broadcast announcer, the fighter pilot the listener, and the jammers, ground or airborne, the interferers.

While in radio jamming it was the direct signal

which had to be made unintelligible, in radar jamming it was the reflected signal, the far weaker echo, which had to be rendered indistinguishable on the face of a cathode-ray tube. A radar set sends out energy pulses and receives their echoes from bodies in their path, and the receiver, to detect the much weaker reflected pulses, has to be sensitive; it is thus liable to pick up extraneous transmissions on its frequency. The provision of those extraneous transmissions was the function of R.C.M.

A counter-measure of very great importance was the paper-backed metal foil known as 'Window'. Of size appropriate to the wavelength to be countered, and dropped from aircraft, it gave strong radar echoes, and these, at any rate to inexperienced observers, resembled aircraft echoes; thus a few aircraft could give the initial impression of being many, while many, all discharging 'Window' at a high rate, could saturate the defences and so conceal themselves. 'Window' could be used for exploitation or interference.

Other activities became inevitably involved with R.C.M. as time went on. The attack on the enemy defence system had to be complete. Links which were not dependent on radio became more vital as the scale of R.C.M. mounted, and these, virtually proof against jamming, were more difficult to deceive. The hearing and sight of ground observers, the Observer Corps, and the sight of the fighter pilots themselves, must be made to lead to false conclusions. 'Window' dropped from a few aircraft might give a false or obliterated radar picture, but it would not fool an Observer Corps, and for them a confusion of noise was sometimes tried with, perhaps, a Mosquito bomber force passing above a small special force of heavy bombers which was circling and progressing slowly, or flying lower than usual; our hope was to delay the enemy's understanding of the bomber plan and to gain for the main force at least another few minutes immunity from interception.

The enemy fighters, even if the jamming of their radio was severe, were still dangerous, for they would see the opening of an attack from afar and some would be able to reach it before the bombing had finished. Once there, the more experienced among them could pick out the bombers in the glare of the fires or from a chance sighting of exhausts or with their radar, the efficiency of which might have been reduced but not nullified by jamming. A plausible and well-timed diversionary attack with many target markers and some bombs for realism (and some of our fighters patrolling, as it were, in ambush) might draw some of the enemy fighters away from the main force's target; and such diversions became an essential part of many plans. In this way 'spoof' developed, and in the Group's activities there evolved, besides the pure R.C.M., a make-believe effort, by which minor attacks were disguised as major attacks, turning points on the route of the main force were concealed by a handful of our aircraft continuing on the original track discharging 'Window', or in a similar way feints were made towards likely targets. 'Spoof' went much further, and later on the plan sometimes included flights by training aircraft over the North Sea in full radar view of the enemy, thus giving a good representation of an approaching raid against a northern target, while the main force or forces struck in the south.

R.C.M. in fighter operations has already been described. Fighter radar transmissions could be homed on from great distances (and even if the enemy crews used their gear sparingly or not at all, they would still not be safe from our fighters' radar). These operations, which had showed such early promise, were to be much increased, as were the low-altitude patrols at enemy bases in which the specialist intruder squadrons of Fighter Command had had such consistent and well-won success. The Group's fighter activities also could not be limited to R.C.M. The success of homing depended largely on the enemy, and if he changed his equipment or restricted its use, we also would have to change our equipment or our tactics, and this involved delays. Our fighters had to be versatile, so that they could be kept busy while awaiting new equipment or when the weather ruled out their more usual type of patrol. So it was that they were allowed to chase their opposite numbers at any stage of their patrols, from take-off to landing, or to bomb their hangars, runways and parked aircraft in a general harassing effort.

We hoped that the material success gained in these operations would be more than matched by a lowering of the morale of the enemy crews, and we were not disappointed, for post-war interrogation showed that there had been a great effect. Among enemy night-fighter crews the ubiquitous Mosquitoes had earned an almost mythical reputation and almost every crash was attributed to them.

For success in R.C.M. we required the fullest pos-

sible knowledge of the frequencies and other characteristics of enemy equipment, which we learned from
the usual intelligence, prisoner-of-war reports, airborne
and ground search and, for final confirmation, the
examination of captured equipment. In ground listening stations watch was kept for enemy signals and the
radio frequencies were constantly searched (in the
same way as anyone can search for new radio stations
by turning the tuning knobs of his receiver), while in
the air a parallel effort was maintained, aircraft going
out on most nights far over enemy territory, the observers logging each signal received and determining
its fundamental characteristics (and so identifying its
probable source), or, if appropriate, making record-
ings for replay. The examination of captured equipment gave the final confirmation of what was probably
already known, and since any equipment so hazarded
by the enemy would almost certainly be standard, we
would learn from the examination all we needed for
R.C.M. action against equipment used by a major
part of the enemy force.

The Germans were not inactive in R.C.M., although
in some ways they were, it seemed, far behind us.
Nevertheless, towards the end they had developed,
amongst other things, a damaging system for homing
on our bombers' radar transmissions, by which means
they could detect and home on a bomber from fifty-
odd miles away with no need for communication with
the ground. This interception system was proof against
jamming (for jamming would also interfere with our
use of those frequencies, and we depended on it for
target finding), and since radio search could yield no

clue, it was only reports from prisoners that first pointed to its use. It is noteworthy that here was a significant indication of a trend; it suggested that the pendulum might go past dead centre, that the tables might be turned and the dark become potentially more dangerous to the attackers than the daylight; but with a change in our tactics and equipment the trend disappeared, the cover of darkness still seeming to be effective.

To discharge its rôle, the Group had to apply signals intelligence with a minimum of delay, and had to be strong both in intelligence and signals. It had the services of a small team of scientists and radio engineers, and it controlled a workshop laboratory and a trials flying unit. Within the Group, special R.C.M. equipment could be designed and built, air tested and, if satisfactory, manufactured in small quantities and fitted into operational aircraft. It also enjoyed very high priority in the industrial production field, which ensured the rapid manufacture of urgently needed special R.C.M. gear in larger quantities. Quick action on intelligence, which would save the lives of aircrews, was thus assured.

This outline of R.C.M. covers the field of the Group's ultimate functions and scale of action when it had attained its full strength, sending out a hundred and more aircraft per night. But in December 1943, soon after its formation, the effort was a mere handful of aircraft: a Beaufighter or two, a Halifax or two, a Wellington, perhaps, and nothing more. Much was attempted; what was achieved was at times disappointing and discouraging, because the enemy, ever resourceful and resilient, was able, right to the end, partly to overcome many of the counter-measures applied. But to confirm that the measures taken were successful there was, besides the fact of lower losses, the evidence provided by the Germans themselves after their defeat—and I was fortunate enough to hear it from them.

Chapter 17

THE FIGHTERS

THE Group moved to West Raynham in Norfolk to form, and to wait for a few weeks until the headquarters was ready. We were kept busy taking over five stations and moving in the units transferred to us. Then came their assessment and, here and there, some reorganisation.

These units, though all assigned to R.C.M., were as mixed in character as they were in equipment. There was one flight of Ansons, another of Defiants and Beaufighters, a squadron—the only operational one—of Halifaxes, Wellingtons and Mosquitoes, another squadron of Merlin-engined Beaufighters and some Mosquitoes, two more fighter squadrons with a few Mosquitoes and no adequately trained crews, and finally a squadron due to have Fortresses but with no aircraft at all. Of the three fighter squadrons one had, as I have mentioned, already been operating with marked success, but the others were newly formed and non-operational. All three were to have Mosquitoes, but the only Mosquitoes of the required type then available were coming forward very slowly, as they were replaced in defensive squadrons by machines equipped with the most modern radar, as yet banned from operations over enemy-occupied territory.

Bomber support by radar fighters was new, and in the fourth year of an exhausting war, with all production committed to the hilt, effort had still to be diverted to fitting new Mosquitoes with the obsolescent radar which alone was allowed in enemy air. Yet these aircraft were intended to go far, 500 miles or so, and then to fight it out; and for that none but the best obtainable was good enough.

With the A.O.C.[1] I flew to Ayr, where two of these squadrons were stationed before their move to Norfolk, and we tried to answer the many anxious questions from the temporarily inactive and disconsolate crews about their future in Bomber Command, and in particular their chances of getting the aircraft they so badly needed. The weather closed in and we had to return by rail and road, eventually creeping into West Raynham just after dawn in a thick fog. That same morning a drive for equipment was started which was to slacken only after the defeat of Germany. Here, as elsewhere, the A.O.C. succeeded. Things moved quickly, and in a remarkably short time all the Mosquitoes had been given a major overhaul, re-engined, equipped like those we had at Ford with a second radar transmitter for tail warning, and were provided with reliable homing gear; and before long new Mosquitoes equipped up to this standard were coming off a special production line.

Fighter operations started with the despatch of the remaining Beaufighters and what Mosquitoes could be mustered. A small effort was maintained while crews were being trained and aircraft brought up to operational standard, re-engined and overhauled. Suddenly it began to grow and successes mounted—and

[1] Air Vice Marshal E. B. Addison, C.B., C.B.E.

these were not confined to a few crews. Losses there were, but they were soon overshadowed by the successes; morale and confidence, which had been shaken by inactivity and by engine failures, came back strongly. For one reason and another the losses rate fell, and the small effort, which had had to be kept going, grew. From the beginning it paid good dividends. In those first few months seven enemy fighters were destroyed for each Mosquito lost, and for every one destroyed there were others damaged and many scared—and for each encounter a bomber might have gone unscathed.

Thinking back over my own experiences—those of an average pilot—and remembering how the squadron as a group of people can react to incompletely understood circumstances, I felt satisfied that the Mosquito myth was being firmly established in enemy minds, for their fighters were being caught at all stages of their patrols, and their only safeguard was never to forget that a Mosquito might be following them—and this would seriously reduce their efficiency.

Development was rapid, although at the time it seemed slow. The function of some of the units was changed, as were some of the commanders. Fighter operations were paying, and they were increased after the conversion of one of the squadrons to the rôle of intruding, pending re-equipment with radar fighters. Radar Mosquitoes were confirming their early promise, gaining victories six or more hundred miles from home. There was considerable evidence that enemy radar gave no tail warning; their fighters were still being caught unawares. We had superior equipment, and the success we hoped for would depend largely on the crews—in particular the observers, who now had also to be navigators. Other R.C.M. operations were to develop later, but in the meantime our fighters' reports gave us invaluable information about enemy habits and methods, which we applied in our own fighter planning, where we had a free hand, and also as time went on in the main bombing plans, on which our advice was increasingly sought. The bombing planning was ponderous and the execution resolute. The miracle was performed on most days; a complex plan was worked out in all detail and transmitted to the crews within a few hours. This was very different from the war I had known; in Fighter Command we had always had to be ready for what the enemy might do.

It was new and enthralling to be a senior staff officer in the special Bomber Command Group, but as the novelty wore off I found myself sometimes depressed for more reasons than the inaction inherent in staff work. Occupied with the defence of one's country, it had been easy to overlook the fact that a bombing success often meant the obliteration of a large part of a town with a heavy addition to the general fund of unhappiness and pain; but now one was a closer witness of the attacks, and their significance loomed large. Yet we in the Group were fortunate, since success for us was the survival of bomber crews, escape from what they, in their own apt slang, called 'the chop', and in the nature and intended scope of our work there was a clear-cut mission, the most worthwhile we could have wished for; and I, in my post as Senior Air Staff Officer to the A.O.C. (with which I was given a brass hat, an incongruous though acceptable prize), was doubly fortunate, for I had considerable authority, the extent of which sometimes scared me, and was given great freedom. I guessed rightly that the strongly individual elements of Bomber and Fighter Commands, and the scientists and other specialists of the staff, would be welded into a happy team by our A.O.C.

Rapid promotion (and being a tin god of a sort in the Group) was intoxicating, but if real values were sometimes forgotten the contemplation of a staff officer's work made me stone-cold sober; it was, after all, the aircrew who went out in hostile air. And fortunately there were always the A.O.C. and others who made it impossible for me to retain inflated ideas of my importance. The Group was, in fact, no longer newly formed when I found this message waiting for me in the headquarters: "For Air Commodore Chisholm. Wing Commander Maxwell telephoned to say that he did not *give* you the Auster." This referred to my dilatoriness in sending back to Ford an Auster, a favourite of Gerald's, which I had borrowed about a week before.

We moved from West Raynham to the ugly but well-heated Victorian mansion that was to be our headquarters. It stood in its own grounds about a mile from the road, and the staff lived in huts in the grounds in fair comfort. The surroundings in that flat but attractive county left little to be desired. We were in the heart of the country, and with several small aircraft at our beck and call on an airfield half a mile away, we were completely mobile. All our stations were close, and any one of them could be reached in fifteen minutes. Hurrying over a lovely countryside often *en plein air*, one's scalp being massaged by an eighty-mile-an-hour wind, usually not bothered by radio, extra engines, rectractable undercarriages, or by having to dress up, in most weathers and sometimes in the dark, to attend a briefing, to see a take-off or await a return, to speak with the crews and so to keep in touch—this was the best sort of flying.

One night in March 1944 more than ninety bombers did not return from a raid on Nuremberg. The enemy fighters seemed to have had it all their own way. This was the heaviest loss yet. There were important visitations to the headquarters in search, perhaps, of clues to the cause of this disaster. Enquiries were made about the support given to the bombers; there was a strong case for increasing it.

Among those who were inquisitive about that loss was my host on a Sunday spent near Horsey. He took me to see a Marsh Harrier's nest. He was a great wild-fowler, and as we walked he talked of the bird life of the fens. To a townee wrapped up in a technical war, this was a beautiful vision of another and contrasting world. To live there and watch birds was all that I could then have wanted. But suddenly and embarrassingly I was brought back to the war; my host's bird world was not such a contrast. "I have been meaning to ask you," he said, "what happened that night when ninety-four were lost. I was wondering whether there was any connection between that loss and the light conditions. It was the sort of night I would have chosen for duck flighting." I said something lamely about the urgency of the attack. I knew only too well that those light conditions would have helped the fighters to destroy our bombers, as they had helped us to destroy bombers in 1941 before the cost of operating in moonlight had been learned, and, as my host knew, they would have helped to shoot duck.

The immediate sequel to this disaster was that two more squadrons of Mosquito fighters were transferred from home defence to bomber support, and the short-wave radar which they carried was released for use over enemy territory. Thus the bomber-support fighters acquired a new ability to 'see' at low altitude and over a wide field to a maximum range of five or more miles. This excellent radar, a product of British development and American industry, had the particular virtue of intelligibility in that during an interception the movements of the indications on the cathode-ray tubes were easily translated into a correct mental picture of the actual positions and movements of aircraft. In this respect alone an immense advance had been made; the observer saw the plan position of his aircraft and the aircraft to be intercepted; ranges could be read with fair accuracy at all distances—a view without perspective but more informative than a bird's-eye view. Projecting a beam, this radar could 'see' ahead without at the same time scanning the ground; thus it was effective at low altitude, and the way was opened to intercepting enemy aircraft as they were preparing to land at the end of their patrols and probably short of fuel, their most vulnerable moment.

These two Mosquito squadrons were a potentially powerful addition to the small force of fighters which,

Imperial War Museum

'. . . a potentially powerful addition . . .'
A Mosquito equipped with A.I. Mark X.

'. . . perhaps the fighter that might have attacked them had been caught by a Mosquito . . .' A camera gun picture. The destruction of a Me. 110

(*See p.* 198)

with obsolescent radar or with no radar at all, had been providing the only direct opposition (other than the bomber's own armament) to enemy fighters, but they were far from ready for operations in their new rôle, being in part deficient in equipment and training. Their radar equipment, though excellent, was incomplete. To the rear the aircraft were blind, and blindness, though scarcely dangerous to a Mosquito flying fast, was a practical drawback when one avowed objective of the operation was to catch the enemy fighters approaching or crossing behind. More important perhaps was the effect on the performance of fighter crews of the knowledge that they themselves were not being stalked.

Unlike the earlier marks of interception radar, whose all-directional radiations made a distorted globe-like halo round the aircraft and which received and displayed simultaneously the echoes from any reflecting bodies within range, this newer type, using ultra-short waves and (by virtue of their shortness) a reflector bowl of manageable size, produced a narrow beam which was made to scan the sky by moving the reflector. To the rear the fuselage and engines screen the 'view'; the aircraft was thus blind in that direction.

It was fortunate that we had some time before developed, from the standard bomber tail-warner, a suitable device for these fighters in anticipation of their release for bomber support. Such a device consisted, in brief, of a separate radar set 'looking' to the rear with a separate cathode-ray tube for showing what was 'seen' there. The location of this new tube in the already full cockpit of the Mosquito night-fighter was a matter of concern, and in some trepidation we had it placed so that it could be seen by the pilot, thus allowing the observer to apply his whole attention to what was to be 'seen' ahead. This odd sharing of the radar 'sight' was logical, but knowing the conservatism of aircrew in general and of pilots in particular, we knew there was a risk that they would object to and condemn as impracticable this idea of the pilot keeping a 'look-out' behind and sharing some of the overworked navigator's functions. However, after initial unpopularity, this arrangement was accepted, and later it was acclaimed, so far as aircrew will acclaim an innovation, as the best solution.

Modifications were carried out quickly, for we had parties of mechanics in the group to do the work besides laboratory workshops where the gear could be assembled, and by cramming in 'boxes' (as even the most complex radio or radar unit was called, and these were later to total twenty-five per Mosquito with a hundred and forty valves) the aircraft were made ready.

Another problem was crew training. They had to learn how to find distant patrol areas and, after the confusion of chases and perhaps combats during which the observer-navigator could no longer be navigator, their home bases. Some crews had to be weeded out and others found to replace them. The appropriate and successful experiment was made of introducing some ex-bomber crews to this new rôle. The Mosquitoes with the newest radar began their operating on D-Day, little more than a month after their rôle had been changed from defence, and almost at once the destruction of enemy aircraft began at a good rate.

With the increase in the number of bomber-support fighters another problem came to the fore, that of identification. It was not that there was a risk of attack on our own bombers or even on our own fighters, because the former's size identified them and the latter were equipped with radar which made a surprise approach and attack impossible. The risk was that our fighters would become mixed up one with the other, each trying to get on the other's tail, each failing, each wasting time and each returning with a story of coming upon an enemy fighter with a performance and radar that made the interception inconclusive, a heavy blow to morale. A radar system had been developed and had worked well, giving the long-range identification that we needed, but this was not sufficient by itself, because radar systems were notoriously unreliable and not all our fighters could carry the necessary gear. Recourse was made, as it had been for defence, to infra-red light signalling and, as in defence, it was a success. Its adoption had been a long shot; several of us remembered making the first trials of the system at Ford a year earlier with some misgivings, and it was almost with surprise that we read in reports "the chase was broken off when I got the infra-red signal". By the use of this invisible light, most familiar to the public in burglar alarms, the identification problem between fighter and fighter in the mêlée over Germany in the night air was partially solved, and the efficiency of our fighter effort must have been immeasurably improved. In eighteen hectic months fighters of the

Group destroyed more than two hundred and fifty enemy aircraft, besides probably destroying a further dozen and damaging a hundred and twenty.

There were occasional lulls due to weather or a full moon, when Bomber Command did not operate, and then proposals came in from the stations for Mosquito daylight sorties over occupied Europe. These were executed singly at very low altitude, within easy reach of cloud cover, and had the objective of attacking any military target seen; they could yield good (and varied) results, and so they were permitted.

Headquarters' first reaction was pained surprise. Bomber Command was not used to the solo turns of the fighters, and we were instructed to limit the operational objectives to those directly associated with the counter-offensive against the night defences. Night-fighter bases became the focus of attention, but on the routes to and from them the Mosquitoes continued their total war, attacking a variety of aircraft and land targets. It was understandable that, once over enemy-held territory, crews would overstep the mark, attacking objectives other than night-fighters—and this view must have been taken by Command, for their reports were accepted with tolerance. It was good practice, and such activity was a guarantee of high morale.

One report I remember from a crew which had destroyed a transport aircraft, shot up a train and bombed a ship, read something like this: "We saw and destroyed a Ju.52 full of night-fighter crews; we shot up a train full of night-fighter crews going on leave; we bombed a ship, etc." The last was too much; other people bombed ships and the Navy was concerned, and a ban was imposed on attacking ships, for good reasons which we could not question.

It was at about this time that an approach was made to Bomber Command by the American 8th Air Force with an offer of assistance by their long-range Lightnings (P.38) and Mustangs (P.51), of which they had a large force for escorting their day bombers. I was sent to their headquarters to discuss the operational use of these fighters and to make the necessary plans. It was arranged that a small detachment would be stationed at one of our airfields for training and some operations, on the results of which further plans could be made. A liaison officer for the headquarters would be appointed. This was a characteristically generous offer, and while I had to mention our belief in the indispensability of radar or at least a navigator, I also stressed the astonishing performances of some pilots who had made a speciality of intruding in single-seaters. There were chances. A few days later two P.38's and two P.51's arrived at Little Snoring, and Major Tom Gates joined the headquarters staff. Tom was a fifty-year-old Texan, with a slow speech and an attractive way with him; he attended our planning conferences and listened patiently to discussions on megacycles, wave-lengths and pulse-recurrence frequencies. Then one day he announced earlier than usual that he was going off 'to see the boys', and the next thing we knew was that his name came through on the night's operations programme. Tom was going with the bombers to Berlin in a P.51 to see for himself.

He got there and got back safely, but on his return he strayed over the Ruhr and he, probably the only

Allied airman over the Ruhr that night, got everything
they had. After that we just saw him at the planning
conferences, and then he would be off 'to see the boys'.
He and they did several more trips, but they saw no
opponents and this plucky experiment was abandoned.

Chapter 18

JAMMING AND 'SPOOF'

LATER on, more help was forthcoming for the bomb-ers. Another squadron, converted to the R.C.M. rôle for the D-Day operations, continued to operate thereafter in their support. Its function then had been to jam the early warning radar (to 'dazzle' the enemy's long-range 'sight') completely and on a wide front. To do this its aircraft, each one equipped to jam all early warning frequencies, took up and kept positions chosen to cover all the enemy stations (whose locations and frequencies were known from photographic and radio reconnaissance). Behind this screen our aircraft could approach France unobserved. After D-Day this same technique was used, over the Channel, the North Sea and later over France and the Low Countries, to screen bomber forces or to suggest their approach and alert the enemy defences unnecessarily. Each jamming position in the screen had to encompass the whole range of frequencies used for early warning, and as this spread, so the jamming effort had to be increased; more transmitters had to be carried and more power was needed. Where the Defiant had once carried the necessary jammers, the Beaufighter had next to be adopted, and then, for D-Day, the Stirling, and later two Stirlings or Halifaxes, and finally very near the end when, as a last resort, the enemy started using a few freak stations, three Halifaxes; and where a squadron of Defiants had sufficed, two squadrons of Halifaxes became inadequate.

So did the radio war progress. A frequency was used by the enemy; it was discovered, identified and jammed; other frequencies were brought into use, giving the defence a respite, and then they were eventually overtaken by the jamming; frequencies were spread farther and the jamming effort was increased; more aircraft were diverted to the R.C.M. rôle; the process went on, the frequencies running away from the jamming and the jamming following the frequencies, like wages and prices in monetary inflation.

The jamming spiral, too, seemed to have an inevitable tendency towards a breakdown. The radio effort in night bombing, aimed at keeping the fighters away from the bombers, was becoming more and more expensive. The proportion of the total effort that was devoted to the support of the bomb-droppers was increasing—by the end more than ten out of every hundred aircraft were supporters and not bomb-carriers —and looming ahead was the certainty that the enemy would follow the allied lead to shorter radio waves and mechanically scanning narrow radar beams, with a consequent demand for greater jamming effort. (Most of the sky could still be searched by a narrow beam without serious interference from a jamming effort that would obliterate the echoes produced by a wide beam.) It seemed that night bombing the way we were doing it was nearing the end of its tether, and that the end of the war in Europe, now evidently not far off, was going to come none too soon. What might have happened had not that end come when it did remains an interesting subject for conjecture.

So far as fighter opposition was concerned, the trends were not only towards rendering the cover of the dark ineffective but even towards turning the advantage against the bomber, for while eyesight was used in the ultimate stage of the fighter versus bomber contest, the bomber (and in particular the big bomber) was fundamentally vulnerable. The fighter could always see without being seen, and it was going to become more difficult to prevent fighters making the visual contacts which gave them this advantage. But the pendulum was still swinging, and equipment already in operations when the war ended might have given the big bomber at least a respite. Radar gun-laying, giving the same almost miraculous powers with which anti-aircraft guns later defeated the flying bombs, was already installed in a few bombers several months before the end. This complex of devices did practically all that a gunner was taught to do except pull the trigger, and it could also 'see' in the dark when he could not see, and measure range accurately at all distances. With this range and direction information and a gyroscopic sight that showed the necessary 'lead', the gunner could shoot to hit with certainty at aircraft approaching from behind and well outside the range of his unaided vision.

The advantage in visual ranges conferred on the fighter by the dark would thus have been nullified. It was conceivable that the fighter would have been destroyed even before the bomber had been seen. Initially casualties among fighters would probably have been high, and they would have learnt to attack with greater haste from greater ranges and with far less precision. But with the next swing of the pendulum the fighters would have caught up, and with similar equipment they, too, would have been able to shoot blind. Probably carrying rockets or fixed guns of heavier calibre than the free guns of the bomber, they would have regained the advantage. Visibility ranges, which had dominated the night air war, would then no longer be of importance. The sight would be wholly electrical and, if enough effort was put into it, jammable. More jammers would be carried, each bomber being a small jamming generating station and so carrying a smaller bomb load. The full circle would have been described. Night would have been turned into day (until the jamming was effective) by a series of splendid technical achievements. But there was still one more technical achievement that was necessary. Problems of identification would have to be overcome in these blind-firing contests, problems which would dwarf those we already knew.

It was becoming too complicated—the way we were doing it. Perhaps it would have to be done in daylight or, if the dark was to be used still, by bombers relying for their defence on speed alone.

One result of the invasion of France was to reduce the strategic disadvantage under which our bombing of Germany had been carried out. Before D-Day the enemy had always had ample warning of the approach of a raid, whether the route was over France or the North Sea, and he had been able to deploy his fighters with deliberation, but afterwards the warning was much reduced by the use of routes over the bridgehead. Nevertheless, penetrations had still often to be made far into Germany, and many times the North Sea route had to be used; and occasional heavy losses continued to bring home the vulnerability of the big bomber in the dark and the strategic disadvantage that persisted.

The jamming of the early warning system on a wide front became an important feature of every raid, and it had to be continued on off nights when the weather permitted, so as to alert the defences, keep the enemy guessing and invalidate the presence of jamming as evidence of the approach of a raid. This was a heavy load on our operational resources, but soon, with Germany's defeat imminent, other squadrons were transferred from the bombing force to our Group to help in the protective effort. These acquisitions, though late, were of incalculable value, for with them it also became possible to stage diversionary 'spoof' operations on a small scale. Another invaluable addition to our effort was provided by an American R.C.M. Liberator squadron, whose crews flew regularly in the screen or with the diversionary forces; they did the job efficiently and with a typical minimum of fuss.

It has already been mentioned that aircraft-like radar echoes can be made by metallised paper strips known as 'Window'. 'Window' dropped in great quantities from aircraft circling low and progressing at convoy speed had been used with success at the time of the invasion to present to the enemy coastal radar the appearance of an approaching invasion fleet, and in the following year it was to be used with the intention of simulating big concentrated bomber forces.

Here were opportunities for concealing routes and destinations, and for diverting the fighters' attention. A few aircraft keeping station with space between them for a big force would cross the enemy coast or the front line, discharging 'Window' at a high rate. Such a 'spoof' force might operate alone to alert the defences and provide quarries for our fighters or, more often, in conjunction with a bombing force or forces to draw off the fighters. Alternatively, as part of a raid, the 'spoof' force would break away from a bombing force, feinting towards a likely target or continuing on its original track when a main force turned, or it would first appear in a sector some distance from the routes soon to be followed by the main forces; the intention was always to divert fighters from the bombing forces to the 'spoof' force. Our chances of success had been increased by a change in tactics since D-Day, the usual easy-to-intercept heavy single attack being replaced by smaller multiple attacks.

As time went on, 'spoof' operations became more elaborate. Bombs and target indicators were dropped on diversionary targets, and an ever-growing load of 'Window' was discharged on the route. Often the stuffing was put into these attacks by the Mosquito bombers of another Group; sometimes some of our own fighters dropped bombs before starting their patrol.

All enemy spectators, air-raid wardens, civil defence and observer corps and, most important of all, the fighter pilots, had to be deceived into thinking that the main attack was being made. There had to be target indicators and bombs, so that if the 'Window' misled the ground control, the reports of target marking and

bombing from those on the ground would go to confirm the original false assessment and keep up the
illusion a little longer. And for the enemy fighter
pilots, their radio, we hoped, jammed and useless,
somewhat bewildered and perhaps apprehensive of
being caught by a Mosquito, there were the diversionary target indicators as lures to ensure late arrival
at the main targets.

These small 'spoof' forces were the scapegoats for
the bombing forces. They were drawn from all the
heavy squadrons of the Group, their crews often aug-
mented for 'Window' dropping (an arduous duty) by
volunteer part-trained pilots or navigators, surplus
products of the aircrew training scheme for whom this
was the only chance of operations. They flew to lay
their paper trail not in defence-saturating concentration but in dilution and almost isolated, and thus were
easy to intercept. The jamming would, in theory,
make close controlled interceptions all but impossible,
but it was not without particular anxiety that we
watched the results of the first few operations of this
sort. The hard fact was, however, that if the plan was
to succeed completely, and if the attention of all the
fighters was diverted from the thousand-strong main
force or forces to the 'spoof' force and the latter suffered even total loss, the loss would have been justifi-
able because the fighter opportunities would have been
limited to the twelve to twenty aircraft of the 'spoof'
force (which were all we could muster), while the
thousand of the main attacks would remain unscathed.
This we knew, and although results relieved our
anxieties we knew too—and by a few heavy losses

were reminded—that the risk always remained. These, some of the least known, were perhaps among the finest operations of the air war.

The development of 'spoof' tactics and the independence of bomber groups with their several targets changed night bomber operations. No longer did the main force go out with the fact that it was airborne known to the enemy soon after take-off, its intentions suspected soon after it had crossed the enemy coast, and its target known even before the marking had started, like a boxer going blindfold into the ring with one arm pinioned and the other outstretched. Now the boxer, though still more or less blindfold, at least could use both arms.

In the planning of these operations the Group played an important part, and the response from the other Groups to this upstart authority on enemy air defence was interesting. Some recognised more than others that we were best able to advise them how to reduce the risks of interception, and with those Groups some outstanding operations were staged, in which losses were negligible and everything seemed to have worked as planned.

The 'spoof', to remain effective as a ruse, needed constant alteration and progressive elaboration, and soon this became beyond our own resources. True, training aircraft flew over the North Sea on many occasions to suggest a raid, but the effect of that alone was not lasting and the chances that 'spoof' attacks by our dozen to twenty aircraft, with the few bombs that could be dropped, would be taken as a main attack became smaller as the German operators became more accustomed to their appearance. It was a pity not only that the development of 'spoof' had been late but also that once it had started more had not been added from resources outside our Group to maintain and augment confusion. Our plans often had to remain static for too long; it was only at the very end, when bombs were being dropped on already bombed-out cities, that a small part of the main force joined with the scapegoats in staging a diversion. That combination of a hundred bomb-droppers with the dozen 'Window' droppers had a noteworthy success (later I was able to see the enemy record of that raid) and, though wary by now and loth to leap to conclusions, the enemy accepted it as the main attack and diverted his fighters to it and away from the main force. This success suggested that some small share of the main force's thousand would probably have succeeded in deceiving on the many occasions when our dozen to twenty were ignored.

Nevertheless, once it had started, development had been rapid. The Group had grown, and its strength in flying units alone had risen to six heavy and six fighter squadrons besides training and development flights; from the small beginnings of eighteen months earlier, the operational effort had reached more than a hundred. There was good cause for satisfaction, for much had been achieved. Bomber losses were near vanishing point; the end of the war in Europe was close, and the enemy was unable to put up much resistance in the air. It seemed a long time since ninety-four had gone missing.

It was hard to assess the influence of R.C.M. on this

trend, but the evidence of the intelligence assessments of the raids, coupled with the actual losses, pointed to the saving of a great number of bombers. Crews reported sometimes that they 'never saw a sausage'; perhaps the 'spoof' had worked and the scapegoats had attracted all the attention; perhaps the fighter that might have attacked them had been caught by a Mosquito. The provisional conclusion could only be that many had survived who otherwise would have got 'the chop'.

Chapter 19

POST-MORTEM

THE European War was over and there was a sudden calm. We went to our offices a bit later, we had more time for lunch, and tea became a meal instead of a cup and a bun in an office. Sightseeing flights were planned and final summaries of operations were written. The stations put into action their plans for vocational training and more sport. There was less work and more play, and week-ends became weekends again.

There was little abandon and drunkenness. Why, one might wonder, was this peace taken, to all outward appearances, so calmly and so steadily? Was it that people were tired, all of them, too tired now to want to indulge even in mild debauchery? Was it that they were too concerned about their now imminent futures? Some certainly had need to be, for they had been over-extended, and their chances of finding contentment in the humdrum tempo and questionable value of their peace-time work were small. Some, too, had enjoyed the war. It had been the means for them of getting out of a rut and doing at last something they felt was worthwhile, and they feared a return to the rut. But others were plainly unconcerned; they were ready for what the future held for them, and they seemed to look forward to it. The war, it appeared, had left them unchanged and, once out of uniform, they would doubtless melt insignificantly into the background from which they had come, content with their lot; less imaginative, less impressionable and less critical, they had liked less and disliked less, suffered less and enjoyed less in their experiences; they were fortunate, for their future was assured (and they certainly would not become the last-war-bores, a development probably in store for the others), but they had not had the most from it. So perhaps it was that the European peace was accepted soberly, the steady ones being steady and those who might have led them astray being too concerned about their future to celebrate. The peace-time employment problem loomed large for some. Would moribund businesses rise again? Would it be bearable on a clerk's stool? What were the prospects and method of entry into civil aviation? Stay on in the R.A.F.? Would life abroad again be bearable? What was the aim? Bare security, comfort or luxury? What was one prepared to pay for them? What was the plan to be? These confusing, absorbing and worrying questions were of great concern to some.

It was against this background and in the uncertain period following the occurrence of peace in Europe that I went (in the slang of that period) 'swanning'. But 'swanning', denoting, as it did, touring aimlessly and in some state through liberated or defeated enemy territories, is not a wholly accurate description of my movements, because my tour was anything but aimless. It had as its immediate objective the planning of a visit by an interrogating team to Schleswig, near which remnants of the German Air Force and its High Command had come to a final halt. The enemy forces had been split into a northern and a southern part. In the northern, which had come to rest in Schleswig-Holstein and South Denmark, there were formations ranging from the Luftflotte Reich, the operational command for all units in Germany, through fighter division operational headquarters (the equivalent of our fighter group headquarters) and fighter squadrons down to radar stations, Observer Corps posts and control centres; in fact, the whole defensive system was well represented. They were all there, from Generals to N.C.O.s, ready to give us their view of the radio war, to speak about their difficulties and the steps they had taken to overcome them, and to show off the equipment they had used. The despatch of an interrogating R.A.F. team drawn from those who had been most involved in this last phase of R.C.M. was an immediate necessity, since the Germans were being rapidly removed to prisoner-of-war cages, where they and the stories we wanted would be lost. So it was that Tom Traill [1] and I set off, not strictly 'swanning', for Schleswig.

We chose a track that took us over the most bombed centres, Essen, Hanover, Bremen, Hamburg and Kiel, and flying low over those had-been cities, we saw a shambles that we guessed would well outlast us. On our arrival, Schleswig seemed still to be in the hands of the Germans. It was surprising to see there, on the airfield, as many of their airmen as we would have seen British airmen on any British airfield, and it was as strange to be saluted on leaving the camp by armed German sentries, or to see German officers still

[1] Air Vice-Marshal T. C. Traill, C.B., O.B.E., D.F.C.

driving freely about in large cars, as it was pleasing to be addressed by the waiter in the hotel used as a R.A.F. headquarters as 'Herr General' and to hear the heels of the German batman click as we entered. But a moment's reflection, when amid all that strangeness a moment's reflection was possible, explained their presence.

Their defeat was complete, but they had not been annihilated, and a childhood's picture of utter defeat (which my war had scarcely changed) remained unfulfilled. Instead of having suffered some kind of fate as being swept off a cliff into the sea or, at least, being put to flight and fleeing in disorder into obscure distances, these remnants of once mighty forces had simply come to a stop in Schleswig-Holstein and Denmark, and were waiting for the next steps in some semblance of order, well fed and apparently well provisioned, taking orders from a High Command that now took its orders resignedly from the Allies. The atmosphere was unreal, and a sinister touch was added by the presence of Himmler, still at large in a nearby wood, the luggage in the hotel bar of a suicide Nazi Minister, and the little Belsens, where those who were later to become known as Displaced Persons existed in conditions of semi-starvation.

We fixed the arrangements for the party's visit, made a quick tour of inspection of the German aircraft parked on the airfields, and left for home the next day via Lüneburg, where we stayed the night.

Immediate pre-war air force messes, permanent buildings for an élite on which much faith was pinned, were, in their styles, revealing. In contrast with the

restrained club-like comfort of our messes here, at
Lüneburg the G.A.F. had luxury which suggested an
hotel, and where we had been forbidden a bar, the
G.A.F. had a medieval-style beer cellar with, con-
veniently, a vomitorium in the lavatory next door
complete even to two stone handles for the greenhorn
Nazi aviator to grip or hang from.

A team of twelve was picked and, after initial discussions about the interrogations, it moved to Schleswig in two Halifaxes. We were installed in the Stadt
Hamburg Hotel, which served as a R.A.F. headquarters and mess, and I requested the presence of
two competent German officers from the Luftflotte
Reich, to whom I could explain our requirements.
They appeared on time and we sat down round a
table. I began to describe the object of our visit, and
to tell them what we wanted to know and whom and
what we wanted to see. I mentioned the Group from
which most of us had come, and from their exclama-
tions and from the knowingness of the glances they
exchanged, it was evident that they realised exactly
what we wanted. These were signals officers, and they
had been, in part, directly responsible for the radio
and radar of Germany's air defence, our main target
for the past eighteen months. It was understandable
that they were keenly aware of us, and that they
should show immediate interest when the identity of
the team was disclosed; and it was not surprising to
find later that a close study had been made of the
Group even down to the compilation of dossiers on its
senior officers.

The Luftflotte Reich had been mobile during the

retreat, living, working and fleeing in caravans, and it had come to its ignominious final stop in a pine wood ten miles or so outside Schleswig. It was to this pine wood that we set out on the next morning, in a caval-cade of German staff cars driven by Germans. It was raining, and a ragged mist was hanging in the wood. On either side of the rides along which we drove were caravans drawn back among the trees; but the place seemed deserted. Then, seeing a group of German officers waiting outside a mess tent, we drew up and got out. They saluted smartly and, hesitating suffi-ciently to acknowledge their salutes, pleased to be wearing a best blue and heavily braided brass hat, I led our party into the tent. A long table with chairs on either side divided it into two. Members of our party filed in and arranged themselves, standing, behind one lot of chairs. The Germans followed, ranging themselves behind the chairs opposite. We were ready and sat down. The Germans remained standing, and I signed to them to be seated.

We spent all day with them and we learnt much of value. The questions and answers followed the planned course more or less, but we often went off at tangents when some mutually absorbing point came up, and then there was a tendency for both sides to relax and talk more as technicians, the professional interest supervening, than as victors and vanquished. They were generally co-operative. Most of them were ordinary-looking men, and I had to keep on remind-ing myself, so mild did they seem, that they were the hated Huns and that any one of their number might have been a Himmler. One, their chief spokesman, reminded us forcibly of what we had been fighting for. He coincided closely with my mental picture, from nearly six years before, of all Nazi pilots. His face was scarred and his hair was cropped, and he had a nervous trick of unendingly manicuring his hands. His answers were short, curt and staccato; he had a dull look in his eyes that disappeared once when he spoke of a certain Major Schnauffer who, for destroying more than 120 bombers, had been awarded the highest order of the Iron Cross—"mit Brillianten!" he added, his piglike eyes opening wide—and again when one of our team, well versed in German Air Force personalities (having spent much of the war interrogating prisoners) let slip, with intention, the nickname by which he had been known in his last squadron. Translated, it was 'the last Prussian'. His eyes sparkled, his poise now gone, and his face lit up with a mock modest smile. He was glad to have had such a name, glad we knew he had had it, glad to have earned it. Then his poise returned, his face set again, and the manicuring of his well-kept hands began again. I think we were all pleased that he would soon be on the march to a prisoners' cage.

We learnt that petrol shortage had crippled their defence, and that in the last phase their nightly maximum fighter effort had been limited to about eighty instead of the 200 sorties possible earlier. 'The last Prussian' took pains to explain that this was the main reason for the failure of the defence to shoot down more bombers, but when the questions became more particular regarding the effect of the various countermeasures and subterfuges that had been employed, we got all the clarification we needed on the reasons why the eighty had not had more success. Item by item their difficulties were admitted and some revealing remarks were let drop.

We had a list of specific enquiries to cover inexplicable events and known gaps in our intelligence, and it was one of the former, reported by Ken Davison,[1] which could not at first be answered.

Both sides were using radar identification, their fighters using transponders whose function was to transmit pulses automatically on one frequency when 'interrogated' by pulses received on another. The former pulses would be received where the first pulses originated (on the ground or in the fighters), and they could be displayed, superimposed on the 'blip' of the aircraft, thus showing it as friendly. Being direct and not reflected signals, they were still strong at fairly long range, and in 1941 Gilfillan[2] had shown us that a transponder on Middle Wallop airfield could show us our bearing and distance to base; and from here radar beacon navigation had developed. We found radar beacons invaluable, and it was puzzling that the enemy did not seem to be using them; and then one night in 1944 Ken found one near Hamburg. His Mosquito carried a neat little interrogator by means of which a strong and identifying signal could be extracted from the enemy transponders which denoted range and, through directional receiving aerials, bearing. His observer got the appropriate signal not far from Hamburg, but they repeatedly overtook its source

[1] Wing Commander the Hon. W. K. Davison, D.S.O., D.F.C.
[2] Wing Commander K. A. B. Gilfillan, M.B.E.

so quickly that they could only construe that it was stationary, in fact a beacon—and from that it was natural to suppose that the Germans had been using radar beacons for fighter navigation.

This was the question we put. Did they use these beacons? No, they did not. Then what could the explanation be of Ken's report? They all looked blank and even disappointed because, except for 'the last Prussian', they seemed keen to help and were obviously interested. And then one, an amiable-looking red-faced man with glasses, slapped his thigh and exclaimed explosively: "Ach Gott Mensch! Das war der Doktor Schmidt."

Dr. Schmidt, it appeared, had shared with many of the crews the theory that our Mosquitoes were using their transponders for intercepting them, but no one in high places would believe him, and so to establish his theory he had placed a transponder in the back garden of his house near Hamburg and waited for the Mosquitoes. We all laughed heartily, even, I think, 'the last Prussian'; I hoped that Dr. Schmidt had been in on that evening.

There had been some rather surprising gaps in their reports, and we left that meeting with the impression that there would be far more to be learned from those who had been in closer contact with the day-to-day operations. In that we were not disappointed.

At a fighter group headquarters we found a closer understanding of, and a greater interest in, the radio war as it had affected them, for the men we questioned had had the nightly task of collecting all the clues, sifting them, hazarding an estimate of Bomber

Command's intentions, and making the best use they could of a depleted and harassed fighter force. With some pride they described how the case was built up. Radio intercepts from Britain indicated the amount of day flying going on, and so the weather: weather over Germany would also show the probabilities of an attack. The habits of Bomber Command would be considered, and so an idea could be formed of the probability of a raid. Reports from radar stations of jamming were taken as a signal to alert the fighters, a fact of which we were well aware and which we had repeatedly tried to exploit, sending out jamming aircraft when no bombers were to follow. Some—and we heard many individual theories, of which not all were reconcilable with fact—held that the position of the screen of early-warning jamming aircraft helped to show broadly the probable line of approach of the bombers, but it was admitted that the front was broad, very broad, and that on it enemy equipment was effectively blotted out.

To help overcome this blindness at long range they had developed and used a few special radar sets operating on frequencies outside the standard band. These they used literally to have a peep, switching on for a few minutes, having a look and switching off, so fearful were they that the transmission would be received and identified by our search aircraft and later jammed —for, it was added with a smile, the R.A.F. in its jamming was always a little ahead of the G.A.F. in its introduction of new equipment, a significant and gratifying exaggeration.

No stone was left unturned in their search for clues

as to Bomber Command's activities and intenions. The transmissions of the bomber's own radar search gear —H2s—were listened for and used for determining their whereabouts. A force setting out from England could thus be detected, and it was only in the last phases, when all but complete radar and radio silence was imposed, that little assistance was got from the bombers themselves. But there were other means and they tried them all. They even used the reflections from our aircraft of the pulses emanating from our long-range early-warning equipment, the reflection naturally being propagated in all directions and therefore receivable anywhere within range; and they did all they could to use the heat from the bombers' engines as an aid to interception. Fighters equipped with receivers for infra-red radiations were flying and, in the course of our interrogations, we questioned an observer who had used the gear. He stated that it had a range of five miles—a sinister thought.

There was little doubt that the best had been made of a disastrous situation, and that there were some technical developments which, had enemy industry not been crippled by bombing, would have hit us hard. One was compelled to admire German ingenuity. But the cover of darkness had remained effective right up to the end.

It was apparent that the fighter controllers had often been able to make good general assessments; but while they described with pride the need for weighing up all the clues and making an estimate, the estimate was often, on their own admission, little better than a guess. Among their own comments was that they needed a sixth sense, and one radar-station operator remarked that he had had to be a soothsayer. That they were at times completely misled had been evident from the smallness of the bomber losses and the reconstructions made from the radio intercepts; but we did not expect any candid admissions of this from the operations' staff. We were, however, to get better confirmation than we had hoped for from some records produced by the group commander who, in his anxiety to prove that his group had never been caught out, offered with alacrity to show us a photographic record of a certain raid as viewed from his operations-room.

They had used a neat system for displaying information in their operations-rooms. Our familiar plotting table became a vertical darkened screen, and on it the positions of aircraft and other information were shown by light symbols from a battery of small projectors. These were operated by women, each linked by telephone to a reporting centre. Thus a photograph of the screen would show a large-scale map with various signs giving all the information available about the raid at that particular time. A series of photographs would be the record of the progress of the raid as viewed by the German fighter controller. A small projector was produced, the room was darkened and the film shown. It was plain, when we had seen it, that the defence had not been taken in on that night. They had seen and identified the main force, had correctly estimated the target, and had sent the fighters there in good time; and our losses, we knew, had been heavy. We were interested, and we took the projector and the film away with us. Several days later, when we had returned home, there was time for a closer examination of this film, and in a small drawer in the projector's case we found a further half-dozen films, each of which also registered a raid. We ran them through the projector, and discovered that they gave as good proof of the deception of the Germans as the other single one gave of their perspicacity. This was the best evidence yet. More than one film indicated a heavy raid developing on target A when target B was the real target and was, at that time, being bombed. One wondered whether these films had been overlooked in the chaos of defeat; the acquisition of such evidence in that way was profoundly satisfying.

The scene of defeat was complete. The German Air Force was immobilised. Row upon row of day fighters, night fighters, freighters, transports and bombers stood grounded for ever, mute and useless. I saw, and did not stop, a V.I.P. transport being opened with a pickaxe for the parachutes inside it. There were jet fighters and bombers, in shape well ahead of their time, and some of the freaks which seemed so near to the German designers' hearts.

At Eggebek airfield there were several examples of the Me.163, the small unorthodox rocket-engined fighter, reminiscent of the fairground aeroplane on a child's merry-go-round, on which Hitler had pinned much desperate hope. In one of the otherwise deserted hangars we came upon a German pilot, loafing aimlessly it seemed, brooding perhaps on an uncertain future. He was eager to talk.

Yes, he had flown the Me.163, and to my most usual question, "How many hours?" he replied, I thought somewhat ruefully, "Ten Landings," and I was reminded that the Me.163 had a duration of seven minutes only, that it was reputed to explode on landing if the fuel had not been expended, and that the usual completion of a sortie was by parachute. He spoke with admiration of the aircraft's speed and climb, and he quoted the interception at 30,000 feet of a Mosquito whose vapour trail was seen from the airfield where a Me.163 was ready to take off. It was fortunate for the Mosquito crew that the guns of the Me.163 jammed.

On Schleswig airfield we found a radar-equipped two-seater Me.262 (twin jet) and its pilot. He described the success of this combination against the Mosquito bombers, mentioning that Allied bombing had driven them to operate from an autobahn, and he recounted an experience which had puzzled him. One night, during the customary raid on Berlin, he was rapidly coming up to and was ready to open fire on a Mosquito when it evaded violently and got away; he believed he had hit it. He was sure that the crew had had warning of his approach, and this was unexpected because he thought, rightly, that Mosquito bombers were 'blind' behind. He was uncertain of the date, but I had little doubt that this and the following incident, reported by one of our Mosquito fighter crews, were one and the same.

The Mosquitoes had been bombing Berlin with a regularity which earned the German's description for them, 'The Berlin Express' (and for the routes on which they flew, 'Platform 1, 2 or 3'), and they had been dropping up to one hundred 4,000-lb. bombs per

' Row upon row of day fighters, night fighters, freighters, transports
and bombers stood grounded for ever.'

Imperial War Museum

The Me. 163 showing wheel undercarriage and retractable landing skid

night. The Germans had seemed powerless to intercept them and the losses were very low. Then they began to mount and there was evidence that pointed to fighters finding them. So, one night, a composite force of Mosquito bombers and fighters went out to Berlin.

The operation was uneventful except for one fighter crew who reported that an aircraft had come up behind them, overtaking very rapidly, and that as they turned hard to evade and to try to get on its tail, it had shot at and hit them—and in support was a perforated exhaust manifold. Our fighters were unable to repeat this operation, having to operate with the main force, and Mosquito bomber losses never became serious; but something here had been achieved. A doubt had been sown in the enemy's mind. Had Mosquito bombers now got tail-warners? If they had, then an attack could not be so deliberate; it might be hurried and inaccurate. The situation was not completely understood. It was interesting that the Mosquito bomber, had the Germans not been very near defeat, would have had to replace bomb load, in part, with radar.

In our inspections we came across a Messerschmitt 110 night-fighter, the rudder of which was covered with insignia to mark the destruction of British bombers, each a tiny R.A.F. roundel and an aircraft in plan view. There were 121 such signs, and on each the type and date were meticulously painted in small letters. A German appeared, and we questioned him about this aircraft. It was, he said, that flown by the Geschwader Kommodore, a Major Schnauffer, the pilot for whom 'the last Prussian' had shown such admiration.

He was here, the ace Schnauffer, waiting to be interrogated. Our informant turned out to be a night-fighter observer who had used in operational trials all the latest gear the Germans had. He described the infra-red receiver, and told of its ability to pick up an aircraft at five miles. When asked whether he had tried to intercept the moon (the infra-red radiation from the moon had sometimes complicated our trials at Ford), he replied in the affirmative, adding a graphic description of a lengthy and exciting chase which ended in the finding of a large conflagration in the Ruhr, and we all laughed. It was evident that infra-red homing had its limitations, but it seemed that it had not a long way to go before becoming very lethal.

We settled down in the afternoon to interrogate the aircrews, starting with the redoubtable Major Schnauffer, who then claimed to have destroyed 124 bombers. He came in, saluted smartly and was told to sit down. He was a fine, sensitive-looking man, and round his neck he was wearing the highest order of the Iron Cross, a beautiful bit of jewellery studded with diamonds. As from the next day the wearing of decorations would be banned. I felt sorry for him. He had done well for his country and, having been elevated on a pedestal of public adulation that would have turned anyone's head, here he was, beaten down, now to be denied the wearing of his decorations. What, I wondered, would happen to him after release from the prisoners' cage? He would at least have a memento of his great adventure when he had been living on the peaks, an individual above himself. These were the unavoidable sentimental trends of my thoughts, and to redress the

balance it was necessary to remember the indescribable conditions of the Russian prisoners in a camp
within the precincts of the station, for which the ex-
commander of the station was being held responsible.
We were the victors and these, the vanquished, were
all partly responsible for these horrors, excuse themselves as they might. And so my feelings hardened and
I listened to what Major Schnauffer had to say.

He led off with an expression of regret that he had
been responsible for the deaths of so many fine men—
he was shedding crocodile tears—and in that atmosphere it hardly rang true. He insinuated that the contest was unequal and that once the fighter had made
contact the conclusion was foregone. (He claimed to
have destroyed seven and seen many more bombers
on one night.) He admitted, though, that the corkscrew evasive action, recommended to all but unfor-
tunately not used enough by all, was entirely effective
as evasion on a dark night, and he recalled a forty-five
minute chase which he had had to abandon. He showed
a profound knowledge of our equipment and tactics,
and it was plain that he was a master in his own sphere.
A reluctance to be entirely frank on certain plans led
to his abrupt dismissal with orders to appear before
the Allied Camp Commandant at the end of the interrogation. Here he was ordered to produce a written report
and all squadron documents within twenty-four hours.
He was dealt with roughly; our interrogator minced
no words and he was dismissed seemingly scared and
crestfallen. This was a strange situation, and the cross
currents in one's feelings were confusing. But these
were the hated Nazis; so why be polite to them? One

knew that politeness, to put it generally, would triumph ultimately; but why be fussy about it now? Why forget the responsibility of each of these men for the prisoners' camp at the gateway of the aerodrome?

A succession of other fighter crews was dealt with. They varied, as ours did, from dim to intelligent. We obtained further proof, and as much as we could have wanted, of the efficacy of our jamming. Their radar was often useless, and communication with the ground was severely hampered. It was satisfying to find a generally accepted belief in the dominance of the Mosquito fighters, and a real fear that all their radar transmissions were being homed on. Legend had grown up about some of the general 'spoof' tactics, based on one or two recognisable and remembered successes when a bogus target not only drew off the enemy fighters but led to the destruction of some of them by Mosquitoes patrolling there. As we had hoped, such successes, together with intruder successes when Mosquitoes were known to have destroyed aircraft near or even on their own airfields, were magnified; rumour spread and events were elaborated, and eventually every crash was due to a Mosquito, every night-flying accident— of which there were many since German fighters often flew low to avoid Mosquitoes and sometimes hit high ground—was attributed to a Mosquito. We had expected this; in fact we had counted on it, knowing the elaborate effect that the few appearances of intruders or believed intruders had had on our own squadrons. The German crews did not differ from ours, and with frequent reminders of the powers of the ubiquitous Mosquito and its admirable equipment, they moulded

Major Schnauffer's Me. 110

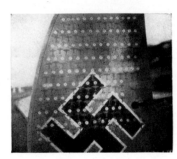

'. . . the rudder covered with insignia to mark the destruction of British bombers. There were 121 such signs . . .'

'A German appeared and we questioned him about this aircraft.'

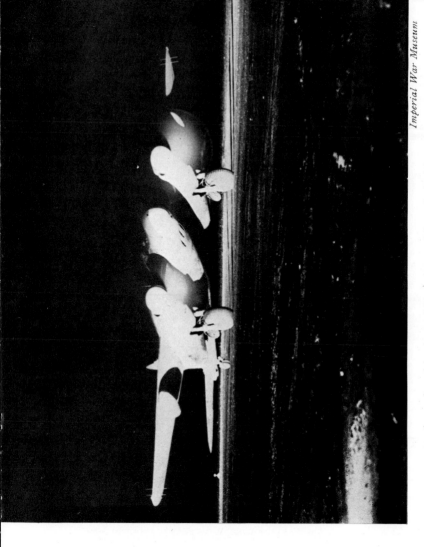

Imperial War Museum

'. . . the ubiquitous Mosquito and its admirable equipment.'

their flying practice as if intruders were ever present. A current description of the safe height for the return to base after a patrol was *Ritterkreuz* height, for that height—they avowed it was only a few hundred feet —had to be maintained if the Mosquitoes were to be avoided and the *Ritterkreuz* won by survival. A homely touch was added by the story that sometimes pilots would go down on their knees and mockingly pray to Goering for Mosquitoes to fly.

We had to make a quick visit to Grove in Denmark before going home, and an enterprising Group Captain of our party mobilised one of the many G.A.F. Junkers 52s which were on Schleswig airfield. In it there was ample space for all, including two German liaison officers.

I was sitting in the co-pilot's seat going over the controls and instruments with the Group Captain who, with one circuit and landing in a Ju.52 to his credit, was going to fly us there (and I was going to try my hand on the way back), when one of the Germans exclaimed, as he got in: "I'm a Junkers 52 pilot." Perhaps he was boasting, perhaps he was only wanting to be helpful or perhaps he doubted our proficiency and was anxious; probably his motive was mixed but, at that time, it was impossible not to play the conqueror and I said: "Now you are going to see what we can do!" He subsided crestfallen and, I have no doubt, anxious as the aircraft trundled off to become airborne almost as soon as the engines were opened up, rising laboriously as a big bird. Thereafter we felt every bump, and watched, fascinated, the flapping of its corrugated wings.

The flight was, of course, uneventful, but on the return the centre engine began to smoke and I throttled it right back and edged towards the main road, for it was about getting a lift back to Schleswig and not about bringing off a successful forced landing that I was anxious, so extraordinarily safe did that twenty-five-year-old aircraft feel.

This brought the post-mortem investigation to an end, except for a visit to Copenhagen to inspect aircraft left there and for some genuine 'swanning'. We had heard all we wanted and we had learnt much of the difficulties under which the German defence had laboured. We were satisfied that the efforts of our crews had not been in vain. Every member of every crew of the Group's motley force, of the Fortresses, Liberators, Halifaxes, Stirlings, Wellingtons and Mosquitoes, could know that his efforts had contributed to the reduction in bomber losses. How great this contribution was cannot be assessed, but those of us who knew the problems of night defence against bombing had heard enough from radar-station operators, fighter controllers, fighter pilots and fighter observers to realise why it was that the enemy had not done better with his remaining fighters. And those of us who had not had the privilege of being airborne and of contributing materially had the comfort and satisfaction of knowing that, though chairborne, we had helped in an unspectacular way.

Chapter 20

MIRAGES

THE post-mortem, complete now but for the writing of the report, marked the end of the war for me; I knew that I was not going on to the Far East. I felt contented and satisfied, as, I expect, most did just then.

In the evening of one of those perfect days which we refer to doggedly as typical of an English summer, I flew back to Norfolk from Schleswig. The air was clear and, ignoring my maps, I headed south-west and then west, keeping, and now and again seeing, the coast on my right. I was alone in a Mosquito, cruising at four miles a minute, and I kept low so as to see as much as I could of the country and the towns that flashed by, for I did not expect to see Europe again in this way.

Such mobility was then intoxicating. Naïvely I imagined a future Europe in which frontiers would mean no more than they did then in the summer of 1945. This excusable vision was parallel in its hopeless optimism to an earlier one suggested by the polyglot fighter squadrons of the Battle of Britain. Thrown together after the collapse of France, Frenchmen, Belgians, Czechs, Poles, Britons and others had flown and fought in perfect and impressive harmony, their aims identical and their understanding effective, thanks largely to the basic English of the radio. Then I wondered whether a happy expedient, possible perhaps only in the R.A.F., would be allowed to last. Was its obvious success not significant for the future? But, sad to relate, it lasted only in a small way, and although isolated pilots and crews remained and others continued to be found in R.A.F. squadrons up to the end, national squadrons were formed and most were gathered to them. So the French and Belgians, Poles and Czechs and others, were posted away and, from being in that close comradeship with Britons that exists between aircrew of the same squadron, they became, when the first difficulty arose, 'the bloody Frogs, Poles, Czechs, etc.' That vision had not lasted.

That same evening, after landing in Norfolk, I was hurrying back to the headquarters, intent only on being in time for dinner, when I was intercepted by a breathless messenger with a request that I would come immediately to the control tower to get in touch with the local customs authorities. I conformed, stating that I had arrived back from the Continent but had nothing to declare; but I was surprised and annoyed, for not only did I feel that this was a premature intrusion (one was not inclined to make allowance for the over-zealousness of a new official or of an older one seeing his first chance in five years), but it was one which brought me back to earth with a bump.

My vision vanished like a mirage. Peace had broken out with a vengeance. My new Europe was still-born.

The report was finished, and I was posted to another headquarters for six months' harassing and interesting work, the nature of which excludes it from this story. On the morning of January 1st, 1946, I emerged from the Wembley demobilisation centre, a brass hat still on my head but a brown-paper parcel under my arm, a civilian again. Some months later I went back to Persia, from where I had started.

FULL CIRCLE

I LAY on my back, my hands under my head, and I stared at the sky. I was in a private cell and the walls were of muslin. This, a mosquito-net, protected me from the insect world, from the marauders whose diligent attacks seemed to be planned, and from those others which, flying blind and with no plan, blundered into and as quickly out of my privacy.

The night was fine and the sky was beautiful; there was a moon and the air was very clear. The coolness of the garden was refreshing; the green things seemed to radiate coolness as the brick walls of the house radiated the day's heat.

I saw the stars in the groups I recognised, and my thoughts switched back to the great days. The stars, the moon, just this clarity of atmosphere. Then, airborne, I was master of the situation. Under my hand was plenty of power; under my finger was the punch that could knock a house down; I was completely mobile, but now I was earthbound and I had to shelter under a net from the attacks and blunderings of the insect world. I was in Persia and it was June. There had never been any doubt in my mind at the time. Those had been the great days and I had been living on the peaks.